Creator's Guide to
Snap Inc.'s Lens Studio

T0106535

TURNER PUBLISHING COMPANY
Nashville, Tennessee
www.turnerpublishing.com

Creator's Guide to Snap Inc.'s Lens Studio

Cover and book design by Archie Ferguson

Library of Congress Control Number: 2022936754

9781684428304 paperback
9781684428311 hardcover
9781684428328 ebook

Printed in the United States of America

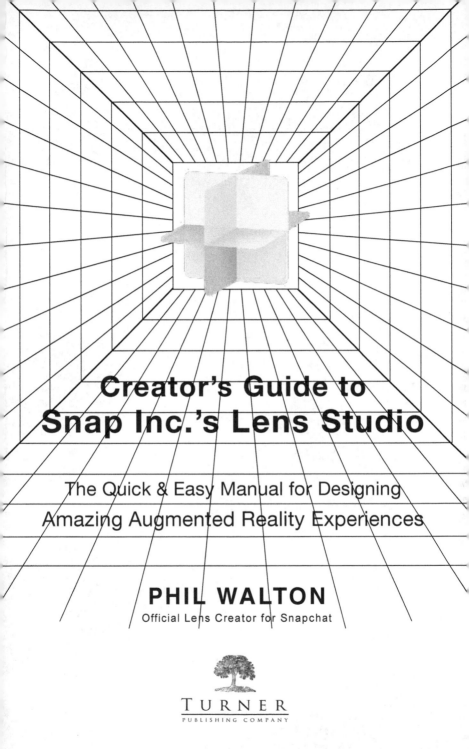

Creator's Guide to Snap Inc.'s Lens Studio

The Quick & Easy Manual for Designing Amazing Augmented Reality Experiences

PHIL WALTON

Official Lens Creator for Snapchat

TURNER
PUBLISHING COMPANY

Creator's Guide to Snap Inc.'s Lens Studio

TABLE OF CONTENTS

Welcome to the future! It wasn't that long ago that phones had cords and rotary dials. Computers took minutes just to boot up, and games came on 5¼-inch floppy discs. When we did finally get the internet, it required a screechy modem that tied up our only phone line while we waited for a simple web page to load. Now we have powerful devices that connect us to the world instantly and that fit inside our pockets. Not only can we find endless possibilities for entertainment, education, and enlightenment, but our smartphones have the amazing ability to understand what's happening inside the image on the screen and add their own new elements. Complex computer-generated imagery on-screen now happens in real time and reacts to our movements. We're truly living in a magical age.

When I started my journey into the world of Augmented Reality (AR), I was trained in 3D animation for television and film but had almost no programming experience. So creating beautiful and complicated interactive experiences seemed to be the exclusive domain of expert software development studios and professional teams of talented people who had all the specialized skill sets to create these things.

Then I discovered Lens Studio. Here was a program that not only allowed me to build my own amazing AR experiences but also let me do it with little or no programming involved. It was easy to use and the documentation was actually up-to-date and helpful. And when I published my effects, within minutes they were readily available to the millions of Snapchat users around the world. I was sold. Oh, and did I mention that Lens Studio is free?

In the time since I first started using Lens Studio, I've learned a lot, had some amazing opportunities, and even had a few of my very own creations shoot to mega-stardom. I'm fortunate to call "Snapchat Lens Creator" my career. It's what I love. I hope I can pass along my knowledge, experience, and passion for building awesome Snapchat Lenses to you. Thank you for your time. Now let's have some fun.

My goal in writing this book is to help the hobbyist or career digital artists who want to be able to create and publish their own powerful AR experiences with Snapchat. As I mentioned in the introduction, I don't come from a programming background. I'm an artist by trade and I'm still on the journey to understanding programming languages like JavaScript (which Lens Studio utilizes). I want this guide to be accessible to everyone, especially those who aren't as versed in some of the more specialized technical abilities that Lens Studio can do. I'll briefly cover concepts like Machine Learning, Programming, and Shaders, but won't be diving into them by any educational depth. Even if you do come from the more technical side, there will be a whole new skill tree to unlock, complementing your existing powers. Get ready to flex the artistic side of your brain as you complete step-by-step tutorials (with downloadable project files) to make your own amazing AR.

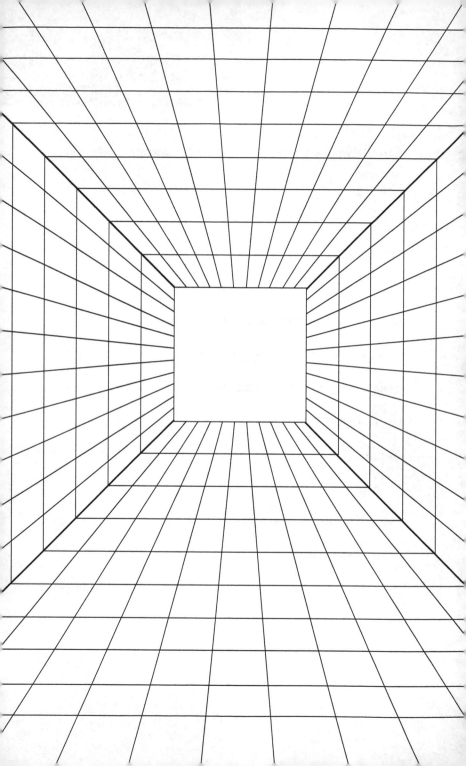

WHAT IS AUGMENTED REALITY?

Since Lens Studio is a platform for creating your own augmented reality, or AR (if you don't want to type out "augmented reality" every time), it would probably be good to know exactly what that is, right? Here's the thing: it's actually hard to come up with a succinct definition of AR because it does cover a lot of territories. Virtual Reality (VR) is typically defined by the user wearing a headset with screens that projects a binocular, computer-generated world that appears three-dimensional. If you've heard the term MR, or Mixed Reality, it's considered where either virtual or augmented reality presentation is combined with live footage. And the entire category of virtual, augmented, and mixed reality fits into the overall header of Extended Reality, or XR.

So, at its most basic, AR is an overlay or alteration of what's happening on-screen with some type of computer-generated imagery. AR is characterized by a mix of real-world and virtual elements; it can be interactive or participatory; and it also utilizes some form of tracking to accurately position those virtual elements in 3D space. For example, when Snapchat puts those puppy dog ears and tongue on your face, it's happening on-screen—it's tracking right with your face and it happens when you open your mouth. That's augmented reality!

Okay, cool. So now you know what AR is, but how does it work? This is where the real wizardry comes in. Modern smartphones and devices use their cameras, processors, sensors, and screens in perfect coordination with one another to produce the AR effects we see. One or more multi-megapixel cameras take in the image. The built-in gyroscope, accelerometer, and even possibly GPS information are all fed into the processor where a sophisticated Machine Learning (ML) algorithm helps your device "understand" the image as a dimensional scene. This algorithm can tell the program where the ground is, or track the parts of a human face. This allows the software to accurately place the computer-generated elements on your high-definition screen. It's the seamless integration of hardware and software working together to create wonder. Do I know exactly how that all happens inside your device? No. I'm just happy I can use it to turn people into talking pickles.

STRENGTHS AND WEAKNESSES

So, just like you wouldn't use a hammer to clean your snow globe collection, AR is a specific tool for solving certain design or technical problems. It's helpful to know what it's good at and what might be better solved with a lint-free cloth and some glass cleaner.

STRENGTHS

- **Accessibility:** AR is easily available on hardware that we carry around all the time—a smartphone or tablet—and is now being built into smart glasses as well. Applications for AR also tend to be smaller in file size to maintain that portability.

- **Dynamic:** AR can add powerful, lightweight computer-generated effects to images and video. It can even use real-world images and geometry to create experiences—everything from a printed postcard to an entire building.

- **Utility:** AR can also understand what's happening on-screen and provide you with useful information in the real world. With sophisticated new machine learning models, you can have AR do everything from recognizing a dog's breed, to letting you do a virtual try-on for an outfit before you buy it, to measuring the actual 3D dimensions of the room you're standing in.

WEAKNESSES

- **Hardware:** A low-resolution camera and/or screen makes for a poor presentation of AR. Any device hardware that's not performing up to current industry standards will have an adverse effect as well.

- **Situational:** Cameras work best when there's plenty of light.

AR requires a good working camera and a proper view of your environment on-screen. Also keep in mind that some AR is pulling data from a server, so it will require an internet connection.

- **Platform:** Most AR experiences aren't coded from the "ground up." They're built on a software framework that does most of the heavy lifting. But not all of these frameworks are built with the same features or abilities.
- **Assets and assembly:** Poor design, low-quality models and art, broken code, and awkward interactive points will all make an AR experience suffer.
- **Education:** There's a little bit of familiarization with using AR that some people just haven't learned yet. But over time, an increasing prevalence and ubiquity will make this less of a factor.

With a better idea of the advantages and drawbacks of AR, you'll be able to play to its many strengths as you create your own experiences. As investment in and use of AR continues to grow, our responsibility as designers will be to do our part to advance the medium.

PLATFORMS

As mentioned earlier, there are a few software platforms that enable you to create AR experiences. Some leverage existing game engines like Unity; others are custom to creating for social media platforms like Snapchat and Instagram. Each has its own advantages and disadvantages. While some require extensive knowledge of programming as well as art, others allow for those with less programming experience to get in and start creating. This isn't a comprehensive list, but here are a few worth mentioning:

- **Lens Studio:** Snapchat's AR creation platform. A powerful and easy-to-use program for creating AR experiences on Snapchat and Snap Camera. Includes a wide range of features from face/body/hand tracking, 3D scene understanding, machine learning, Location Markers, and much more.

- **Spark AR Studio:** Facebook/Instagram's AR filter creation program with templates, asset libraries, and a powerful patch editor system. They have a large and talented community of creators and frequent feature updates.

- **ARkit:** Apple's AR development engine—robust feature set includes Depth API, geolocation anchors, LiDAR support for iPhone 12, motion tracking, and more.

- **ARCore:** Google's AR engine meant for building simple and powerful AR.

- **Vuforia:** AR engine that uses the Unity platform. It specializes in image marker and model tracking. A solid programming background and knowledge of Unity are required.

- **AR Foundation:** Unity's AR Development platform is designed for developers with core features that easily deploy to multiple mobile and wearable platforms.

- **Adobe Aero:** Basic program for displaying AR objects in 3D world space.

Lens Studio

The focus of this book will be on Lens Studio, free software released by Snap, Inc., specifically to enable creators of all skill levels to produce and launch Lenses (which is the preferred nomenclature for AR experiences on the Snapchat ecosystem). I've used other AR development software and this is my personal favorite. For people like me who have a design-focused background, it makes the creation process very easy to go from start to finish on an AR experience and have it quickly published to the world. The features are robust and constantly improving. And the resources—including tutorials, documentation, and a friendly creator community—are exceptional.

DEPLOYMENT AND DISTRIBUTION

It is important to remember that as you are designing your AR experience, you have more than one avenue for distribution.

Snapchat

This is the primary avenue where your Lenses will be seen and enjoyed. With a user base of around 250 million, Snapchat encourages users to discover and try new Lenses. With the Lens Carousel and Explorer, they're constantly recommending fun new Lenses to try, which helps creators like us get our work out to the world.

Snap Camera

Any face-based lens can not only be used on Snapchat but also on the webcam-focused Snap Camera program. Snap Camera came into popularity with the movement of workers from in-office to doing work from home. It's since gone on to become a very popular engagement tool for Twitch Streamers and YouTubers. Download Snap Camera free for Mac and PC (sorry, no Chromebook version) from snapcamera.snapchat.com.

Spectacles 3

Snap released these specialized pairs of sunglasses with a built-in camera on each side, which captures and interprets depth in video footage. In Lens Studio, you are given the ability to publish Lenses specifically for Spectacles 3 footage. These Lenses utilize the depth information captured by dual-camera Lenses on the Spectacles 3 glasses and apply the lens to the captured footage after the fact. Learn more and purchase your own pair at spectacles.com.

Spectacles (2021)

Recently launched AR glasses have built-in screens for displaying the experience. Spectacles (2021) allow the user to have live, real-time, and hands-free (or interactive!) AR experiences.

Snap Kit (Creative Kit and Camera Kit)

While more of an indirect distribution option, the toolset for Snap's

Creative Kit and Camera Kit allows for some really unique options for custom branded Lens experiences outside of the main Snapchat ecosystem. These make it possible to integrate Snapchat functionality (like AR Lenses) within your own mobile app. How cool is that? I won't be delving into Creative Kit and Camera Kit in this book, but there are some great examples and more information on the Snap Kit website (snapkit.com).

Making a good AR experience comes down to the convergence of creative design, technology, and storytelling. The inspiration can come from anywhere, but for a really good experience, all should be working in harmony. Here are a few things to keep in mind:

CREATIVE DESIGN

Our job as designers is to add order, understanding, and beauty to the world. It's helpful to keep principles of good design as you construct your AR experience. Your creative design should factor in the context of the experience. Where will someone be using the AR? How are you expecting them to interact with it? What will they see, hear, and experience? What are your interaction points? How will they be triggered? How do they find it in the first place? And as you're considering that, don't forget about the audience themselves. Who is this experience for? Why them? What are you trying to communicate with them?

After you answer those questions, plan it out. It could be a sketch drawn on a napkin, User Experience flow wireframe, full-color concept art, or even storyboards, but having a visual representation of what you intend to create can be a helpful guide toward your end result.

Your design should be one that maximizes the strengths of AR and justifies why you're using AR for this project in the first place—versus another medium—as well as what it looks like, what it does, and who it's for.

TECHNOLOGY

Sometimes the technology itself is the focus. Every time you see an experience that makes you say "How'd they do that?" it's usually a technology innovation that's pushing the leading edge of what's possible with AR. Machine learning models, LiDAR, body tracking, and better scene understanding are opening up amazing new powers for AR. The key to unlocking a new ability is figuring out the best use for what you'll do with it. Just because a feature is available doesn't mean you should make an experience that shows it off. Think about how to make it a complete experience and not just a cool tech demo.

Because AR is typically a lightweight mobile experience, designers should be judicious about how they streamline the experience for file size and attention spans. It should play well on whatever device without lagging or loss of fidelity. The experience should have minimal load times. It should not have any part that feels "broken" due to code that's not acting properly. The overall experience should be optimized so that the user doesn't even have to think about the technology behind it and can simply be wowed by the experience.

STORYTELLING

AR experiences are visual, temporal, and even interactive. This allows for entirely new forms of storytelling. In a very real sense, it brings the user in and makes them a part of the story. Typically, AR experiences tend to be short form, lasting anywhere from a few seconds to several minutes, but it is still possible to deliver an impactful message that connects you as the designer to other people around the world.

There are points I like to consider when I'm crafting a story experience.

UNIVERSAL

We're not so different, you and I. Tell a story that is accessible to everyone (or at least as many people as possible). We all share common experiences and themes in life. Speaking to those can help your story connect with more people.

SPECIFIC

Stories are more than "someone goes to a place and does a thing." The details matter because that is what makes the story come alive and feel real. Specificity says that you have a clear voice and know exactly the story you want to tell.

PERSONAL

Give an authentic voice to your experience. This is the story that you want to tell, after all. Make someone else care about it as much as you do.

ENGAGING

There are millions of things vying for someone's interest at any given moment. And we all have only so much time on this earth. The fact that someone has chosen to give you their time is a true honor. Make the most of it. Attention is a valuable commodity, so don't waste it.

These are simply my guidelines for what a good experience should be, but the rules are not hard and fast. I even find that many of the same creative principles for film and video games apply to AR experiences. Keeping your audience at the forefront of your mind as you go through each part of the design, construction, testing, and deployment process will help your AR experiences be second to none. And don't neglect to get some friends or family to try out your work before you put it out there for the world. They can be very helpful in catching things that you hadn't considered, or determining if some part of your experience isn't working as you'd expected.

THE PROCESS: HOW I WORK

I'll admit that I'm a sucker for learning about famous and visionary thinkers and how they work. I don't know if I expect to learn some secret insight that makes me a thousand percent more productive or if I'm just curious to learn about one of my idol's idiosyncratic quirks in the process as they made that thing that I love. Did you know that to keep himself from procrastinating while working on Star Wars, George Lucas released ten large spiders in his house every day? Okay, that's actually not true, but you never know what new things you might learn from someone else. Here's the thing though: the best process is one that helps you successfully complete the thing you're working on. So here's how I do it:

START WITH THE END IN MIND

Whether I'm just building something for myself (and my fans) or I'm working for a client, I always want to begin with a clear picture of what the final experience will look like and what it will do. That's just a good habit for any designer, so expectations of results can be in line with what comes out on the other side. To that end, the more you can conceive, sketch, storyboard, User Experience flowchart, or even just have a really concrete idea, the better you can execute on the final version.

PLAN THE ATTACK

Once you've got the idea that you want to execute, your next step is to plan out how you're going to accomplish it. What assets will you need to build? What artwork? Will there be any coding or scripting needed? What can you source and what are you actually going to need to make? Are there any templates available that you can build from?

I admit it: I don't know what I'm doing sometimes. I'll get an idea or be asked by a client for something that I'm not entirely sure I know how to do. That's actually okay. The real secret to being creative (and probably just a human) is being able to figure it out. Sometimes I'll go into the documentation on Lens Studio's website or the forums, which are both great and I highly recommend them. Other times I can reach out to the Lens Studio community, who are super helpful as well. And sometimes, I still don't have any solid answers, but at least I have a direction and some theories of how I think it could possibly work. With my best assumptions assembled, it's time to get to work.

BUILD QUICKLY

Artists and software engineers are alike in a lot of ways, but one key difference (in my experience) is in the actual building of the project. Artists and designers can spend a lot of time agonizing over every tiny detail in a presentation, pushing points until it's perfect, but one thing that I've learned from working with programmers is that it is better to get a working prototype on its feet as quickly as possible. I do this because I see an AR experience as a program first and a piece of art second. I want to know early if something doesn't work or any of my assumptions made in the planning phase have been incorrect. I'd rather have that happen before I've put a ton of time and effort into building my assets.

TEST AND REFINE

With a working prototype, it's now time to try it out—see what works and what doesn't. Does it move like you're expecting it to? How do your assets look on-screen? Take notes as you go so you don't forget anything. The great thing about Lens Studio is that it's very easy to swap in new assets and have things still work. So go back and polish up your experience until you're happy with it—or until it's due to the client.

GET FEEDBACK

Unless you're the most self-assured auteur who knows exactly what they want and will settle for nothing else, then it's probably good to get feedback on your experience. Let someone (or several someones) you trust test it out and ask them specific questions. Did everything do what it's supposed to? Did they understand what the experience was about? What did they really like? What could be improved? It's good to know if something doesn't work from either a creative or a technical perspective before you put your work out there into the world.

And remember to let your feedback friends try it without your explaining, making excuses, or apologizing for it. When your users across the world try your AR experience, you won't be there to give a disclaimer.

LAUNCH THAT BABY!

Finally, when you're (reasonably) happy with it and everything is working as it should, it's time to get your masterpiece out there for the world to enjoy. That's the whole point of this creative endeavor anyway, right? Use it, share it on all your socials, ask your friends and family to try it.

And don't get discouraged if you're not getting millions of views right away. That doesn't mean you didn't make something awesome. Move on to your next experience and keep doing the work. Before you know it, you'll have random people reaching out to you to let you know how much they liked that thing you made.

Finally, I want to briefly address perfectionism. It's really easy to look across the internet and find work that's better than yours. That happens to the best of us. But don't let that dissuade or discourage you from putting your work out there anyways. Even if it didn't turn out exactly as you imagined it would—creative work seldom does—the important thing is for you to get your voice, your passion, your beauty out there. And if you still want to go back and make tweaks and changes to your experience after it's launched, Lens Studio makes that easy as well.

So how do you feel? Motivated and ready to start building your own Lenses? Let's get into it. The first thing you need to do is download and install the proper version of the Lens Studio program for your operating system, either Mac or PC. It's available for free by going to lensstudio.snapchat.com. There you will also find the system requirements necessary to operate it. Lens Studio recently reduced its memory footprint, so you won't be required to have as much space available for installation.

Once you have it installed, open the program and sign in to your Snapchat account by clicking on the yellow "Login to my Lenses with Snapchat" button.

Once you enter your username and password (as well as your two-factor authentication step—because you're all about keeping your Snapchat account secure), you'll be prompted to give permissions for Lens Studio to connect to your Snapchat account. Hit Continue and you'll be good to go.

Do You Need a Snapchat Account to Build Lenses in Lens Studio?

Yes. A Snapchat account is now required for the latest version of Lens Studio.

Pairing Your Device

Even though Lens Studio has a preview panel that shows you what your experience will look like on several devices and screens, nothing is better than testing your Lens on Snapchat itself. To do this you'll need to pair the Snapchat account on your device with Lens Studio.

Hit the Pair Your Device button and a large Snap code will appear. Open Snapchat on Your device and scan the Snap Code by getting it in view and doing a long press on it. A prompt on your screen will ask you to pair with Lens Studio and hit the Pair button. After a few moments, if successful, you'll get a green checkmark confirming the Device Paired in Lens Studio and the button will now say Send to Snapchat.

Now with Lens Studio installed, your account logged in, and paired with Snapchat on your device, you're all ready to start making awesome AR experiences.

SOFTWARE VERSIONS

Note that in this book, we will be using Lens Studio version 4.10. Because Lens Studio is software that's in active development, new versions may have come out by the time you're reading this. New features, changes to the layout, workflow improvements, and even bug fixes could have happened in the intervening time. Even with changes, the core functionality and principles will remain the same, so you should be able to get up to speed with whatever version you are on.

Lens Studio is a stand-alone program that contains everything you need to build incredible AR experiences. From the templates to Lens Studio's built-in asset library, there's a lot you can do with what's already there. But as you get more comfortable with the program, I'm sure you'll soon be wondering how to build all the other amazing things you're imagining. For that, you'll most likely need other programs to help you create the design assets that will be used. If you're a working design professional or even a student, you may have access to many of these programs already, but I'll talk about what I currently use and offer some free alternatives as well.

Let me give a disclaimer that I don't personally use the free alternative software mentioned, nor will I be including any specifics on how to use them in my tutorials, but I know other Lens creators who use them frequently and swear by them as a no-cost alternative.

2D ART AND ILLUSTRATION

Adobe Photoshop
It goes without saying that Adobe's Creative Suite has become the industry standard for making and editing 2D artwork. I'm constantly using Photoshop for creating or editing texture files, making 2D backgrounds, and, of course, designing my lens icons.

Free alternative: Gimp (gimp.org)

Illustrator
Used in making vector graphics and illustrations.

Free Alternative: Inkscape (inkscape.org)

2D ANIMATION AND MOTION GRAPHICS

Adobe After Effects
Great for making high-quality motion graphics. I use this for creating 2D image sequences for animated textures and backgrounds.

Free Alternative: Natron (natrongithub.github.io)

Adobe Animate

Those of you who are old enough to remember the program Flash will recognize this. Once the industry standard for creating lightweight 2D animation for the web, it now lives on as Adobe Animate. Great for creating image assets and sequences with that signature cartoony "Flash style."

3D ART AND ANIMATION

Autodesk Maya

A powerhouse 3D modeling and animation program. I use it all the time for making my 3D models, rigging, UV texture layout, animation, and exporting as a usable format for Lens Studio. The big downside to Maya is that it's too expensive to have just for learning purposes.

3D Studio Max

Very similar to Maya (in fact, they're both made by the same company), this has many of the same tools and options for creating 3D models.

Cinema 4D

High-end 3D software that's not made by Autodesk. Frequently used in motion graphics and graphic design for its quality renderer.

Free alternative: Blender (blender.org)

Mudbox and Z-Brush

These are a set of 3D model sculpting programs, which have a different workflow from programs like Maya or Max. They work more like how a sculptor would work with a ball of clay, rather than cutting and manipulating geometric shapes. These programs are great for making detailed organic-looking creations.

ADOBE SUBSTANCE PAINTER

My absolute favorite for making great-looking textures for 3D models. Includes a free library of additional textures and export settings for

Lens Studio as well. Substance painter will provide you with the color, normal map, and material parameter maps texture files used to make your model look amazing.

WEBSITES

Perhaps you're looking for more "off the shelf" assets that are already made. If you do download and use any other person's creative work from one of these places, make sure you comply with the terms of use posted on their website.

Here are a few suggestions of where you can find additional art assets:

Stock Photos and Illustrations

Getty Images, Shutterstock, iStockphoto, and *Adobe Stock*. If you're looking for a particular image as a reference, pattern, or even background, these are some of the main sites for finding a good variety of stock images.

3D MODELS

My two favorite places to look for 3D modeling inspiration are Sketchfab and TurboSquid. Both sites have great examples of professionally produced models; some are even free to download. Since AR experiences are more akin to a video game, we'll want to be looking for models that are optimized for file size and will work well on a mobile device. These 3D models will have a lower amount of geometry—called Low Poly—and have smaller and fewer texture maps.

Although I build my own 3D models for my Lenses, there's actually a lot you can learn from looking at other people's work—everything from how they handled model topology to what they actually built with geometry versus what they've handled with a texture map. There's a real art to making quality Low Poly models and a lot of crossover skills that apply to an AR Lens creator.

Ultimately, the quality of the AR experience you create will come down to the quality of the assets you're using. That doesn't mean that spending lots of money on high-end creative software is required.

They're just tools to help you, the designer, make your thing. The more you know about the tools available and how to use them effectively, the better you'll be able to do your job.

Some of the greatest art ever created was done so with limitations applied to how it had to be made, and yet the end result was a masterpiece. Michelangelo's painting on the Sistine Chapel had to be done painstakingly overhead, and the production of the movie *Jaws* suffered multiple mechanical shark breakdowns—but both resulted in what this author argues are unparalleled artistic contributions to humanity. All that said, you, too, will be expected to work within some technical limitations as you make your Lenses. I have no doubt that you'll be able to use those restrictions to still make amazing art.

It's good to consider these things before you go through the process of building an entire Lens that will inevitably be rejected. Here are a few restrictions you need to factor in when you're designing your experiences. Failure to comply will result in either your Lens being taken down or not being able to submit it in the first place:

FILE SIZE

Every lens must be under 8MB (recently doubled from its original 4MB) before it can be uploaded. Machine learning Lenses have an allowance for up to 10MB total size, factoring in the additional size needed for the ML model.

SUBMISSION GUIDELINES

It may not be a big list, but the submission guidelines set some clear and important boundaries on what is not acceptable in a Lens experience. These restrictions are actually helpful for keeping Snapchat a welcoming and inclusive place for all Snapchatters. Keep in mind that users as young as thirteen have accounts on Snapchat and even younger kids play with Lens experiences on their parents'/siblings' Snapchat accounts. Let's make sure our Lenses are fun for everyone to use.

Here are a few things to leave out:
- Violence, gore, and disturbing imagery

- Nudity and sexual depictions, explicit language, and paraphernalia
- Harassment or bullying of any kind, including doxxing or directing insults at an individual person
- Realistic weapons or violence against people, animals, or self-harm
- Promotion of illegal activity or substances; includes regulated industries like alcohol, tobacco, and gambling
- Hate speech, hate groups, mocking or hurtful stereotypes of any group

Intellectual Property

Don't include any of Snap, Inc., branding, logos, name, or imagery in your Lenses—this includes the word Snap. Also, do not use other copyrighted brands, logos, music, and other creative work in your Lens. Disney, DreamWorks, and Viacom are very protective of their intellectual property.

Additional Technical Requirements

- Frame rates above 27 fps on iPhone 6 (and newer) and 15 fps on Galaxy s6 (and newer)
- No texture maps above 2048x2048
- No models above 100k triangles for unrigged models (60k tris for rigged models)
- Not consuming over 150MB of RAM
- Supported video is under 10 MB, MP4 format with H.264 / AVC codec, smaller than 1280x1280 and resolution in multiples of 16
- Contain no major code errors

Additional Creative Considerations

Here are a few more pointers on how to keep your Lens from being rejected:

- Don't include your username in your Lens (this includes your preview). Additionally, don't add a "Subscribe to me @" or "Follow me for more Filters" message in your Lens. First off, it's tacky, and second, Snap is cracking down on that.

- Don't use images you don't own the rights to in your previews or icons.
- Don't submit the unaltered templates (including mine) as your own Lenses.
- Don't submit anyone else's unaltered Lens project as your own.
- Make sure your Lens works for everyone in terms of age, status, skin tone, body size, ability, and language.

PROGRAM LAYOUT

Before we get into building actual AR experiences, let's take a tour of the Lens Studio interface, so you know where things are and what they do. We won't talk about everything in every detail, but covering the key knowledge you'll need to get around the program and build Lenses. One great thing about Lens Studio is that there are often multiple ways to accomplish an action or several places where you can change a setting. The way I'll be showing you will reflect my own workflow, but you may find other, better, faster ways to do the same thing. Learn the ways that work best for you.

For complete and comprehensive information about everything in Lens Studio, go to lensstudio.snapchat.com/guides.

HOME SCREEN

When you open Lens Studio, this is what you see first. Here we have easy navigation for kicking off a new project or jumping into a previous one.

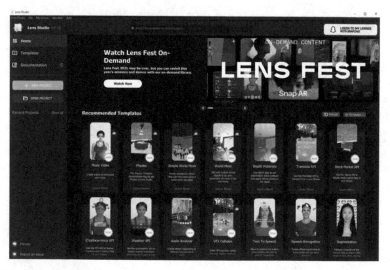

Login Button

Connect your Snapchat account to Lens Studio. You can log in here from the home screen or do it later from the main screen.

My Lenses

Once logged in, the Login button changes to show your profile image and becomes a link to the online dashboard where you can publish and manage your Lenses.

Updates Banner

Featured news, new templates, and other important bulletins from the Lens Studio team.

Recommended Templates

The latest and greatest Lens templates for you to try. Hit the "Learn More" button to get more details about the template or a link to the guide on Lens Studio's website.

Templates

All the Lens templates are listed here, including frequently used ones.

Documentation

Takes you to the Lens Studio site for more information on all things related to the program.

Forum

Managed and curated by the Lens Studio team, with top-tier advice from the experts and fellow Lens creators. It's a great place to ask a question, make a suggestion, or get help with a Lens problem.

Report an Issue

If you find a bug or something is going wrong with Lens Studio, they want to know about it. Reporting issues helps the software get better for everyone using it.

PROJECTS WINDOW

Open a new scene, template, or existing project and you'll be taken to the part of the program where the construction actually happens.

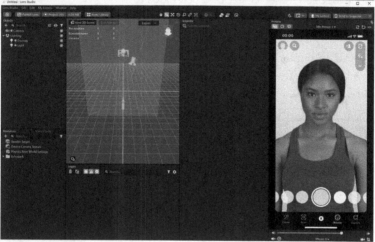

Top Menu

Across the top are the typical menu items for file loading/saving, edit, and help. Others worth noting include:

Lens Studio

Here we find Preferences, where you can set your default project location, change backup settings, and switch off things like "Auto Switch 2D/3D in Scene panel" and "Auto Compress Textures," which I like to have manual control over.

Tool Bar

Also across the top is the Tool Bar, which gives quick access to project settings and other important tools.

My Lenses

Yet another way to get to the online Lens dashboard. Also, an option for logging out of your Snapchat account from Lens Studio.

Windows

Access to every panel in Lens Studio. Especially helpful if you accidentally close one out. Also, a way to reset the panel Layout back to its default, which is helpful if you accidentally "tear off" a panel and are having trouble getting everything back in the right place.

Home

Back to the home screen, in case closing Lens Studio directly is too harsh and you have to ease your way out. I get it.

Publish

When you're ready to launch your Lens experience to the world. We'll learn more about this very important button in the section on publishing your experiences.

Project Info

Set up your Lens icon, preview video, Lens name, experience hints, and specify what type of experience that it's created for (i.e., Front Camera, Back Camera, Spectacles). We'll talk a lot more about this in the publishing section as well.

Lens Size

How many megabytes your Lens is and some tools for improving it. Even though you've got 8MB to use, it's good to make sure your Lens performance is optimized.

Asset Library

An awesome resource for pre-built specialty assets to add some extra wow to your projects. Everything from 2D & 3D models, materials, tools, VFX, Snap ML, audio, and scripts. We'll dig into this treasure trove later in the book.

Navigation
Tools for moving and manipulating assets in the scene view. Contextually switches depending if your scene is in 2D or 3D mode.

Panels Dropdown
Same options as in the top menu.

Pair your Device
Link Lens Studio to Snapchat on your device, so you can send work-in-progress Lenses to test out.

Send to Snapchat
Once your device is paired, this button sends your current work-in-progress Lens to your Snapchat so you can try it out on your device.

OBJECTS PANEL

The Objects panel holds everything that's actually used in your Lens experience. You can add new objects with the + button or drag in assets you have in the Resources panel. Once you have assets in your object panel, you can left-click + drag to reorder or parent objects under each other.

Render Order
By default, assets in the Objects panel are automatically evaluated and rendered in hierarchical order starting at the top first and going down, so things at the bottom of the list appear in front of everything else. While 3D objects are rendered based on their position and depth, render order matters much more for 2D elements. In "auto" numbering mode, you can change render order by changing its position in the hierarchy.

Render Layers
Assets in the Objects panel can also be assigned to different layers. Layers come in handy if you want assets to render together inde-

pendently of other assets. Most commonly, whenever you are adding a new camera to a scene, you'll create a layer for that camera and assign the objects that you want to be seen by that camera to the layer. While scene objects can only be assigned to one layer, both lights and cameras can be on multiple layers.

> **Pro Tip:** Display Mode
> *Switch between Default, Layers, and Render Order view for the Objects Panel to facilitate quick editing of layer assignment and manually setting render order.*

Manually Setting Order

Objects in your scene default to the "auto" render order (based on their place in the hierarchy), but you can manually enter what order you want for each object. Remember that any layer still set to "auto" below in the hierarchy will automatically change to the next integer after the object above it. And you can also manually set multiple objects to have the same number; they will use their order in the hierarchy to determine their render order.

Enabling / Disabling Objects

You can turn off an object while still keeping it in the scene with this check box or use the keyboard shortcut (H). I often use this for testing, setting up scenes, or working with code. Note that disabled objects still count against your overall Lens size.

> **Pro Tip:** Options Panel Right-Click Submenu
> Shortcuts in Lens Studio are an absolute lifesaver. Right-click on an object in the Options panel and you'll get some very useful commands. Here are a few important ones:

Import Object

Pull in a new object directly to your scene (adding it to the Resources panel as well). Shortcut Ctrl + Shift + I or ⇧⌘I

Export Object

Saves your selected asset from your scene as a .lso file, which can easily be reused in other Lens Studio projects. The great thing about this is that it saves not only the object itself with all its settings but any children in its hierarchy, materials, textures, and their configuration as well. Highly useful if you've built something that you want to reuse in another project or if you find yourself constantly setting up the same objects a certain way when you're building multiple Lenses.

Save as Prefab

Prefabs package up objects and their associated hierarchy into neat little instances, which save a ton of space in your Lens and let you do other cool things like spawn and control them with code. So instead of making multiple copies of the entire hierarchy, they just reference the original.

Camera Hover All

Pulls the camera back to frame everything in the Scene panel (Shortcut key A).

Select Subtree

Select your current object and everything below it in the hierarchy.

Create Selection Set

Saves a bunch of time if you're adjusting multiple items at the same time. Select them once and create a selection set. Then you can right-click and easily select them again from the selection setlist.

Group

This parents everything you've selected in your scene panel under a new scene object. Shortcut Ctrl + G or ⌘G

SCENE PANEL

The Scene panel is the 2D or 3D space where you'll build your Lens. If you've used 3D software, this view will be very familiar. Here you'll find the visual version of the assets from the Objects panel ready to be placed and positioned in your scene.

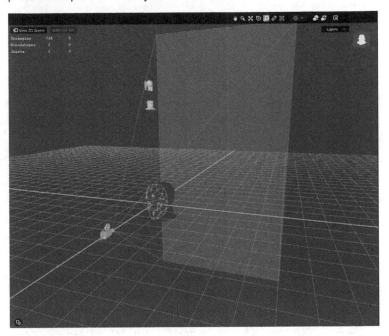

The first thing to know is how to navigate in the Scene panel. Change your view with Camera Movement tools that use the following key-board + mouse shortcuts.

Scene Movement
    Camera Pan: Alt + Middle Click (+ Middle Click)
    Camera Rotate: Alt + Left Click (+ Middle Click)
    Camera Zoom: Alt + Right Click + Drag or Scroll Wheel
    (+ Middle Click + Drag or Scroll Wheel)

Object Movement Tools
   Selection: Q
   Move: W
   Rotation: E
   Scale: R
   Frame Selection: F   ⌥
   Isolate Selection: Alt + Q (+ Q)

Now that you can get around inside the Scene panel, here are a few other important things to know:

View 2D/3D Scene Toggle: Switch the view between 3D and 2D mode. Lens Studio defaults to automatically switching depending on what you have selected.

Layers View: Allows you to view all layers in your scene or isolate just the one you want to focus on.

Scene Camera Orientation: This gives you a visual representation of your orientation in the scene. You can click + drag to reorient, or even click on a side of the cube to quickly jump to a view from sides, top and bottom, or front and back.

Home View: This resets the camera back to the starting position.

Panel Settings: Turn on and off guides and other parts of the Scene panel. The really important feature here is the option for turning on Occluder visualization, which normally appears as a lack of object in the scene. I'll explain why this is helpful later.

Counter: This helps you keep track of how many polygons, blend shapes and joints you have in a scene. Remember that Lens Studio does have limits, so it's best to keep your 3D objects optimized for maximum performance.

INSPECTOR PANEL

The inspector panel gives you detailed information about each item in your scene. With it, you can specify precise values on your assets and even add additional components to it. Simply select an item in the Objects or Scene panel and the Inspector will show you its attributes.

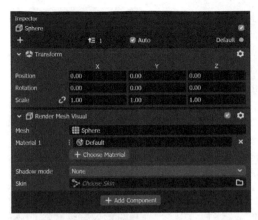

With an object selected in the Inspector panel, at the top you can see an object's name, the layer, and render order. Every item in your scene will have its own transform component that cannot be deleted. Selecting [Add Component] will bring up a large submenu of additional components you can add to an object. At a more advanced level of Lens Studio, you can learn what each component does and even be able to build your own from just a scene object. But for right now, the important thing to understand is that each object in your scene is made from components, which you can edit their data in the inspector panel.

RESOURCES PANEL

The Resources panel acts like a folder to hold any asset you may be using for your project. Everything you import to Lens Studio gets checked (often optimized) and stored in the Resources  panel so that as you build your experience, the assets you need are ready for use.

To add new resources to your project, just hit the + button in the Resources panel.

Lens Studio provides a bunch of different useful assets for building your experiences, organized by type. There's a lot here and I won't break down each one, but as you build more complex projects and examine the templates, you'll start to pick up on which assets you'll need for the Lens that you're working on.

Finally, to import your own assets, hit the [+ From Files] button and locate your files on your hard drive. Or you can also drag and drop them from your computer into the Resources panel. Depending on the type of resource, Lens Studio may prompt you with some additional import settings to optimize the asset.

Pro Tip: Housekeeping

It's a good idea to create folders in your Resources panel to keep your project organized. That makes it much easier to find things—especially if it's months later. I like to organize by the type of asset—so, Models, Textures, Materials, Scripts etc. You should also be in the habit of renaming assets in the Objects panel hierarchy as well. A well-organized project is one that you can hand off to another designer and they can easily see where everything is.

Once you have items in the resource panel, you can right-click for some additional menu options.

A few that you may find yourself using frequently are:

- Update from Source: If you're already using this asset in your project and you change something with the original file, use this to re-import the file, keeping everything in your project the way you had it.

- Relink to New Source: Swap out one project asset with another. This works great for switching 2D art files.
- Find Usage: This will expand and highlight where a particular asset is being used inside your Scene panel.

Warning regarding Update and Relink to Source

These functions are both highly useful and will save you from having to rebuild an entire Lens project from scratch when all you needed to do was make an update. However, with more complex assets, like rigged 3D models with blend shapes, the more changes you've made to the original file, the more likely you are to run into complications with updating and relinking. Lens Studio does its best to match up your new file with the settings of your old one, but the greater the difference, the more likely it will have issues upon import.

PREVIEW PANEL

The Preview Panel is just what it sounds like—a preview of what your Lens experience is going to be like. This panel gives you options to view your Lens on different models, poses, and devices. You can even use your webcam or import your own videos to use as your preview.

Scene Config Panel

The Scene Config panel controls the outputs of your Lens—what gets seen and recorded in Snapchat. Set the camera render order and specify which render target is live (what you see on screen) and capture (what gets recorded) in your Lens—and they can be different.

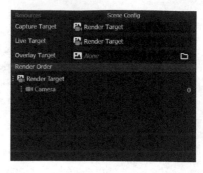

Render Targets

With render targets, you're creating outputs for your lens. You can layer and combine render targets with each other (like adding a background to a 3D object), use a render target to create a more sophisticated alpha channel/segmentation texture, or use multiple render targets to create cool VFX. It's important to remember that render targets must have a camera assigned to them in order for them to work.

I do recommend that as you try out the Lens Studio templates, you also take a look at how they have their render targets set up, which will give you deeper insight into how you can use them to your advantage. You can quickly see what any given render targets are displaying by assigning them to the Live Target.

Capture Target: What Lens Studio records when you're taking a snap

Live Target: What you see on-screen, which can include UI elements or other things you don't want recorded in the actual Snap

Overlay Target: Used for displaying overlay elements for Spectacles (2021) Lenses.

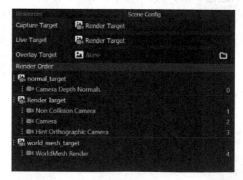

This is an example of a more sophisticated lens that uses multiple cameras and render targets.

LOGGER PANEL

Anyone familiar with web development or programming will immediately understand the utility of the Logger panel as a debugging tool. It gives you status messages for the state of your Lens and Lens Studio. Even if you don't know much about coding, you can still see errors and hints for the scripts you're using listed here. It can be tremendously helpful if you're running into issues.

SCRIPT EDITOR PANEL AND SCRIPT VISUAL EDITOR

Lens Studio also has a lightweight Script Editor that facilitates easily modifying a script on the fly when you're working on a Lens.

The Script Visual Editor is for those of you more familiar with the patch/node system of programming. Less typing is involved and more connecting modules to other modules.

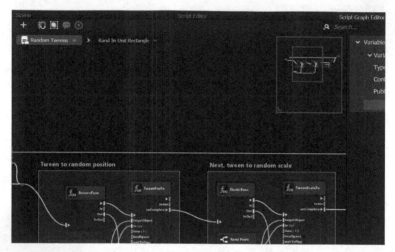

MATERIAL EDITOR AND VFX EDITOR

Works in the same way as the Script Visual Editor in that you're connecting nodes, only here you're building custom materials and visual effects.

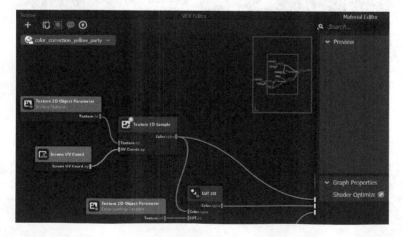

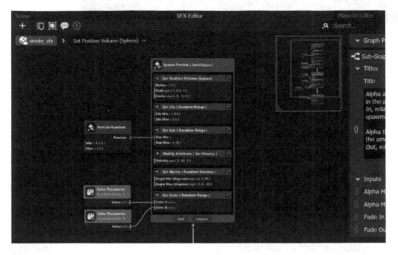

Summary

Some of these panels you'll be using a lot more than others, but it's good to familiarize yourself with them. As you explore new templates and projects, you'll be able to know where to go and what you need to change in order to build your intended experience, eventually gaining mastery over all parts of Lens Studio.

When you find one that's of interest to you, hit the Learn More button to bring up a larger description along with a link to the Lens Studio video tutorial, which is good to watch or at least keep handy if you get stuck. When you're ready, hit the Start Project button.

The template will open and you'll be able to explore in greater detail how they build this Lens. Creative assets are typically nested under the camera that they share a layer with. Expand the hierarchy and take a look at what's in each. Templates often contain multiple examples within the structure that are not visible. Click the Enable checkbox to activate them (don't forget to deactivate the ones you're not using).

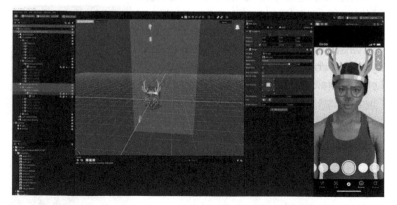

In the Objects panel you'll see the various pieces used to construct this 2D Object face lens. Some are empty objects used for grouping and organization. Beneath the Camera object you'll see the Face Retouch group, which has a Face Retouch object under it.

Face Retouch

This component is a general beauty enhancement modifier used to smooth skin, whiten eyes and teeth, and sharpen the eyes. Computer-aided beauty ethics notwithstanding, I think these are nice to add to a face Lens with just a slight amount of adjustment because the high-definition cameras on our devices today tend to amplify the details a little too well, and it's okay to soften the reality just a touch.

Below that you'll find the 2D Object Examples [Remove_Me] group. This is where you'll find the actual art components used in this template.

Head Binding

This handy component is used to attach a digital object to the user's real head. Head Bindings come with a dropdown menu of different attachment points, or you can move the child items to make your own custom bind point.

Face Occluder

When you create a new Head Binding, it comes with an accompanying face occluder. An occluder is more about a lack of a thing than a thing itself. It is, in reality, an invisible piece of geometry that hides or blocks the digital assets on the opposite side of the face, giving the illusion that the computer-generated object is actually an integral part of the world.

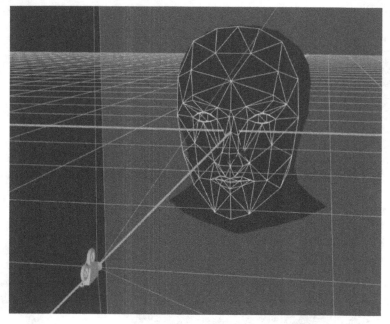

Face Index

Any component or object in Lens Studio that tracks individual people will have a face index number with it. This is a way of assigning different effects to multiple people within a scene. Because this is an index, the first person will be Index 0, second will be Index 1, and so forth. There's not a hard upper limit for how many faces that can be tracked, but performance will probably suffer if you set up face effects for twelve different people in one Lens.

Finally, you have the actual creative assets used to augment the reality. These are "children" under the hierarchy of the Head Binding so they track with the user's face relative to the specified bind point.

Image Object

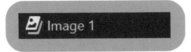

The image object is actually a container that holds a texture in the hierarchy. Use the move, scale, or rotate tools to adjust it.

That covers all the basics of what's in this particular template. I'll let you explore the others on your own and see the different kinds of features, modifiers, and objects available to you. The Lens Studio documentation (https://lensstudio.snapchat.com/templates/) is an excellent guide for how to use each one, and I don't need to repeat their efforts. The best thing you can do is try them all out. Select individual objects and play with their settings to see what they do. This really is a process, so give yourself time to learn.

LIKE A VERSION

Before you get into building, I wanted to drop a quick note about versioning. It's a good practice to be in as you work—especially as you hit project milestones—to save a "current progress" of your project and then start a new version from that save point. For me, I always add a "_V01" to my starting project, then when I version up, it's just doing a Save As and calling the next one "_V02". You may have a different way you want to track your versions, but I highly recommend you save new versions as you complete sections of the Lessons. It's nice to have a save point where you can go back to when everything is working, especially on the more complicated projects, where things might get messed up and you don't want to redo the entire Lesson.

PROJECT 1: 2D FACE OBJECT—LIME HAT CAT MEME

https://turnerbookstore.com/pages/lens-studio-projects

Estimated completion time: 2 hours

What I recommend doing when you first start creating in Lens Studio is taking existing templates and modifying them into an original Lens. There's nothing wrong with this approach, so long as you're using your own artwork when you publish it. The key benefit is that the template is already a fully functional project, so everything should already be working in the project. Also, you get to see how the project is constructed and what goes into building it—which is crucial for creating more elaborate AR experiences.

This first project will be broken down into three lessons: modifying the 2D face template, creating a LUT, and adding script-driven screen text.

MODIFYING THE 2D FACE TEMPLATE

Let's begin with how to import artwork and make your own version of a 2D Object Lens. This gives you the building blocks for any number of face-tracked Lenses. We'll start off slow and easy on this one as you get a feel for everything in Lens Studio.

The first step is to open the 2D Objects template in Lens Studio. Then you can import the art files that I've provided—or use your own if you like. Simply select the art files and drag them into the resources panel. (.PNG with a transparent background is the preferred format.)

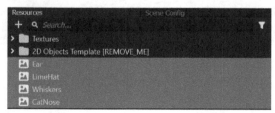

Then in the Objects panel, use the Enable checkbox to disable the other Binding objects, and other art objects—everything but the Purple_Ear so we can just focus on that.

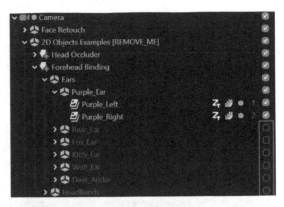

Next, we'll find the image objects in the hierarchy that we're going to be swapping out. In the 2D template, they're named Purple_Left and Purple_Right. Select Purple_Left in the Objects panel.

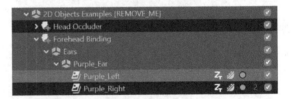

With it selected, drag and drop the file Ear from the Resources panel into the Texture box to replace ear_purple_long.

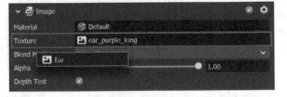

You'll see in the Scene panel that our new ears are in place. They're probably not in the final spot where we want them, but we'll reposition them in a bit.

Finally, rename the Group and the Images in the Objects panel so we stay organized and know which ones we modified. Select the item and hit Enter to rename.

Let's bring in the Lime Hat next. We'll replace the Rainbow headband this time. Start by making sure it's enabled.

This time, with the Rainbow image selected in the Objects panel, go to the Inspector and click on the Texture box where it says **headband rainbow**. That will bring up a Resources panel window where you can select the **LimeHat** file and hit **OK**.

Be sure to rename the Rainbow headband as well before you move on.

Now, let's take a minute to resize and reposition the images so they fit the face better. You can manually position the assets in the Scene panel and enter in precise values in the Inspector panel.

We don't want our image objects to point at the camera. So as we update them in the Inspector panel, make sure the "Align to Camera box" is checked off.

Align to Camera

Now try this process on your own with the nose. See if you can replace the dog nose with our own art asset. When you're done it should look like this:

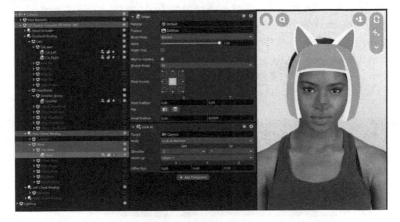

Now let's look at how to add your own images. Select the **Left Cheek Binding** and **Right Cheek Binding Groups** and delete them.

In the Objects panel, **hit the + and add a Face Image** from the Face Effects column.

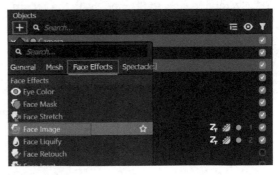

That's going to give you a new Effects group, Head Binding, and Image object at the bottom of your hierarchy. Select the Head Binding and **make sure that the binding point is set to Face Center.**

Then select the image object and set the texture file to Whiskers. Now you can resize the whiskers with the manipulator, but don't move them.

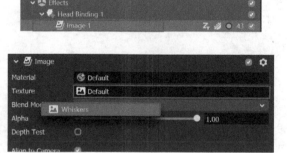

Normally it would be okay to reposition the whiskers right here in the 2D panel, but in this case, that's actually going to mess with our binding point, and we don't want that. Instead, what we want to do is switch to 3D mode and position them with the Move tool (W). (Note: If you do accidentally move the image, select the Head Binding and switch the Attach To Point from **Custom** to **Face Center**.)

Switch the view to 3D mode with the button in the upper left corner of the Scene panel.

And with the Image selected and the Move tool activated, position the whisker image to the side of the User's nose.

Pro Tip: Moving Two-Dimensionally in a 3D Space
You'll notice that the move tool has arrows pointing in the X, Y, and Z axis, which moves the object in that one direction.
But there are also colored squares that you can grab
to move your object in two axes at once.

Position the whiskers where you want them beside the nose. Then hit Ctrl + D to duplicate the whisker image. In the Inspector panel, change the numeric value of the X position to a—to flip the duplicated image to the equal position on the other side.

	X	Y	Z
Position	-5.8726	-5.0546	0.00
Rotation	0.00	0.00	0.00
Scale	9.4032	7.8437	1.00

Finally, we'll use the Flip horizontal button to flip the whiskers in the proper direction.

Don't forget to rename your objects and group—I called the binding Whisker Binding, and named the images WhiskerLeft and WhiskerRight. Then in the Objects panel, delete the parts that you're not using for your Lens, so we are left with a nice, tidy hierarchy.

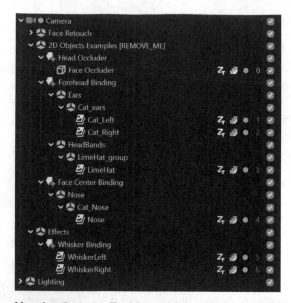

Here's what our final Lens looks like in the Preview panel:

FACE STRETCH OBJECT

Let's quickly add one more thing to this Lens before we move on—a face stretch. These are great for adding some fun face deformations to the user.

Under the Objects panel, hit the + and under Face Effects you'll add the Face Stretch object. Since we only want this effecting the face itself and not our 2D images, we'll drag the newly created Face Stretch object up in the hierarchy, so it's attached to the Head Occluder binding.

In the Scene Panel, and with the Face Stretch selected, we'll view the 2D scene and see a grid overlay on an example face:

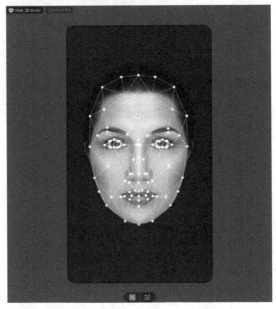

Each of these points you can grab and move to stretch out the face in unique ways. For our purposes, we'll move the points so the user has large cat-like eyes. Make sure the symmetry button is turned on, so both sides match.

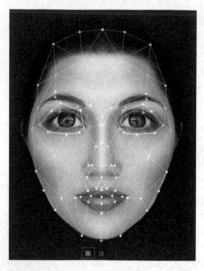

In the Inspector panel, you'll see a slider to change the intensity of the effect and the ability to add more face stretch features on top of your current one. Click the checkbox off and on so you can get a quick before and after for the results of your Face Stretch. And that's all there is to it! Check out the end results in your preview window.

CREATING AND ADDING A LUT

For many just getting started in Lens creation, their first "built from scratch" Lens ends up being a basic LUT applied to the screen. A LUT (if you don't already know) is simply a Lookup Table—it's either a set of numbers or an image that instructs a value shift for the colors in the scene. The results can be anything from a subtle, general boost to the saturation or dramatic complete color inversion. A quick search on the internet can show you lots of available LUTs, even presets and image tables that you can buy, but don't go spending your hard-earned cash just yet.

They're simple to make and easy to apply, but in my view, they do not constitute an entire Lens experience. They're the Snapchat Lens equivalent to what a pickle slice is to a cheeseburger deluxe with fries—an enhancement to the flavor, but not a meal in and of itself.

Let's get into how to add some flavor to our existing Lens experience by creating and applying our own original LUT.

Let's start by opening our reference picture in our photo editing software. In this case, I'll be showing you how to do it with Photoshop and Camera Raw.

Here's the photo that I'll be working with—a handsome man standing in my backyard on a crisp October morning.

A few items to keep in mind for your reference photo:

•   Make sure the photo you are using doesn't already have any color correction applied to it or it will skew the results.

•   You'll want to have a person or multiple people (ideally with different skin tones) in your photo, so you can see the results of your color correction on various people.

•   Try to use a photo with a large spectrum of colors, as well as light and dark areas.

•   The goal is to have an image that shows off all the adjustments you're making as you build your LUT.

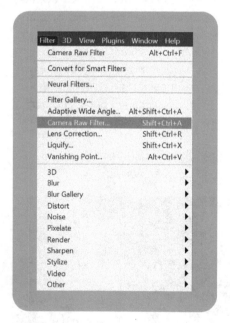

Open the reference photo in Photoshop and then open Camera Raw under the Filters menu.

Next, you'll use the Basic, Curve, and Color Mixer panels to tweak the settings to your liking. Get the photograph colors looking like how you want them to look in your Lens. This can be a subjective process, so I won't be giving you exact values to enter, but play around with it and get creative. The goal is to have clean transitions between colors without artifacting or edges.

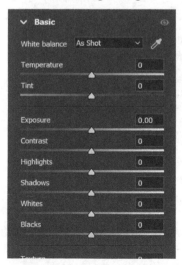

There's an abundance of tutorials online if you really want to go in depth with the process of color correction. For now, just dial in what looks good to your eye and we'll move to the next step.

69

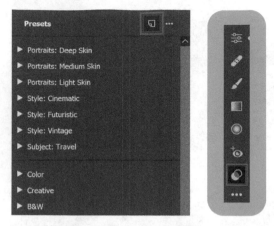

Select Presets from the far-right menu. Then create a **New Preset**.

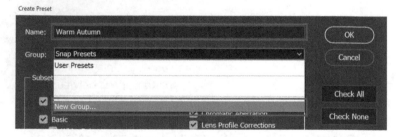

Give your Preset a descriptive name (I called mine Warm Autumn) and I recommend also creating a group for Snap Presets where you can keep your presets organized.

Once your Preset is saved, cancel out of Camera Raw without applying the filter to your image—we don't want to save over the reference photo, because we'll probably want to use it for creating more filter presets later.

Instead, using Photoshop, we'll want to open the basic post effect lookup table available in the provided files or on the Lens Studio website, then activate Camera Raw again.

Then go to Presets again, find the "Warm Autumn" Preset that we created in our Snap Presets group, and apply it to the basic post effect lookup table. Then hit OK.

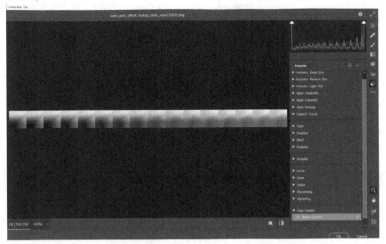

Save the modified basic post effect lookup table with a new name— again, I called mine Warm Autumn. You may not notice a huge difference between the original and the new one, but it will become more obvious when we apply it in Lens Studio.

Back in Lens Studio with our completed 1.1 project open, we're ready to apply the LUT effect.

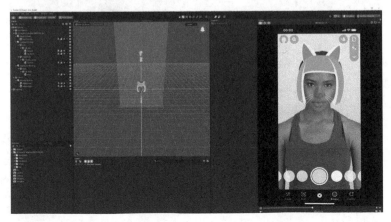

In the Objects panel, create a new Color Correction object—any one will do. For this example, I chose All Yellow.

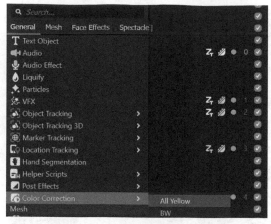

Rename the Color Correction object. Import the modified LUT file (Warm Autumn.jpg) into the Resources panel and then replace its texture in the new Color Correction object we just added. We'll see our Warm Autumn LUT take effect.

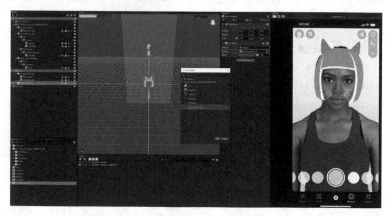

Since we don't want the color correction applied to the other 2D images in our scene, we simply drag it up in the hierarchy, above the other objects.

And that's how you create and apply a LUT!

ADDING SCREEN TEXT AND ANIMATION SEQUENCES

For the final part of this Lens experience, let's look at how to add some dynamic and script-driven screen text as well as a triggerable 2D animation. Sounds fun, right?

Let's start with the project where we left off after we added our LUT. We'll add our text first. In the Objects panel add a Screen Text object.

This will add three new objects to our scene:

1. **Orthographic Camera:** Views the scene without depth and is ideal for 2D presentations.

2. **Full Frame Region:** The container that defines the boundaries where your text object will be displayed. In the Inspector for this object, there's a few options here to keep your text from being hidden by the UI and on-screen for different mobile devices.

3. **Screen Text:** This is where your words go!

Screen Text vs. Text Object

When adding your Screen Text, you probably noticed that there's a Text Object as well. What's the difference? Screen Text is used for putting overlay text on screen in 2D space, whereas the Text Object can be placed in 3D space (if you wanted to pin a word on the user's forehead, for example).

You now have Static text on screen. Whatever you have in the text box will stay that way (unless you use a script to change it, of course). But let's add some Dynamic text instead. Erase the word "Text" in the text box and click the dropdown for Dynamic text. This shows you an array of contextual options to put in the text box. (By the way, you can use Static and Dynamic in the same text box!)

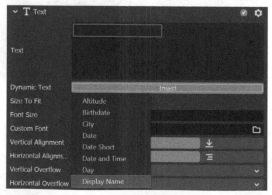

Here we can grab all kinds of information that will show up based on the user. Their city, birthdate, and even weather. Let's select their Display Name. On our preview it will show up as "Snap User," but when we test it on our device it will be our own username.

Next, we'll customize our text by importing our own font file (Impact) to the Resources panel and plugging it into the Custom Font.

Then change the font size to 40, make the Vertical Alignment to Bottom, and add a black outline so it looks like proper meme text.

Finally, in the 2D Scene panel, we'll adjust the bottom edge of the text box up so it's in the proper place.

Now, let's add one more text box. This time we'll use a script to control the text.

Start by selecting the Full Frame Region and add another Screen Text (so our new text object will be within our existing frame region and not in a new one). Then, repeat the Font, Font Size, and Outline customization steps we did for the first text box, so they match.

Change the vertical alignment to Top and resize the text box in the 2D Scene panel for proper placement. Let's also rename our text objects to "Top Text" and "Bottom Text" so we stay organized.

Import and plug in my RandomMemeGenerator.js script available on the website.

Or you can duplicate it yourself by hitting the + in the Resources panel. Add a script. Double-click on the script we just created in the Resources panel, and in the Script Editor panel, enter the following code exactly as it appears (including capitalization):

```
// @input Component.Text text
var randMeme = [
"Has become a cat meme ",
"Is in the limelight ",
"Is not impressed ",
"thinks they look pretty good ",
];

var newMeme = randMeme[Math.floor(Math.random()*rand-
Meme.length)];

script.text.text = newMeme;
```

This bit of JavaScript randomly chooses one of the variables under "randMeme" and assigns it to our text. And if you want you can change the text within the " " quotation marks to be whatever you want, or add your own, following the "your text here" format.

Finally, hit CTRL + S (CMD + S) to save your script.

We'll add this to our project by creating a Scene Object in the Objects panel, and with it selected, dragging our RandomMemeGenerator script into the Inspector panel. Or you can simply (with nothing selected) drag the script to the Inspector panel and it will add it to the hierarchy automatically.

Next, we'll point the script to the text object we want it to change, which is what we're calling Bottom Text.

You will see that if everything is working correctly, the script has immediately changed the words in the text box into one of the values from our script chosen randomly.

This is because we have the script set to trigger its action immediately when Lens is activated. Using this dropdown box, we can actually change when the script is activated. Let's change this to "Tapped" so we can let the user get a different answer if they want. To test this out, click on the preview window and it will choose a different variable from the script.

ACTIVATING ELEMENTS WITH A BEHAVIOR SCRIPT

I want the screen text elements to be hidden when the user first starts the Lens, so this is our opportunity to use the amazingly powerful and versatile Behavior script. For those of us who aren't strong in the ways of JavaScript, this is a great tool for adding interactivity to your experience.

Let's add a Behavior script now in the Objects panel below the Random Meme Generator script. It can be found under the Helper Scripts.

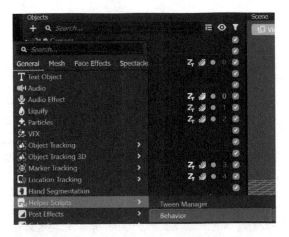

Behavior Script

There's way too much to get into with Behavior scripts in this book. Suffice to say, it's incredibly powerful and versatile. I definitely recommend experimenting with them on your own Lenses because adding interactivity is a great way to increase user engagement with your AR experiences. The important thing to think about when you're using Behavior scripts is:

- What is the trigger to activate the script?
- What object is going to have something happen to it?
- What is the response or what is going to happen?

Being able to answer these questions will help you plan and implement them in your project.

Now that we have a Behavior script in our project, I want to set it up so the screen text starts off hidden and activates when we tap. Our Random Meme Generator script already triggers on tap, so that should work out splendidly.

In the Inspector panel for our Behavior script, we can see that it defaults to a Touch Event for trigger and that Touch Event type is a Tap. The Touch Target is blank, which means the user can tap anywhere on-screen to activate it. This section is exactly as we want it already. What we will be changing is the Response Type. Let's select "Set Enabled" as our response.

Now we can look under the Options for Set Enabled. We make sure the Entity Type is Scene Object and that the action is Enabled. For the Target, we could choose one of the text objects but we'd have to create another for the second text object. In this case, it's simpler to just select the Full Frame Region that they're both under because disabling something in the hierarchy will affect everything below it as well.

Finally, all we have to do to see this in action is to go over in the Objects panel and disable the Full Frame Region checkbox, so that the script can enable the text when we tap. It should also change the text on every subsequent time we tap.

Try it out and make sure it works.

ADDING A 2D ANIMATION SEQUENCE

Let's add one last little touch to this Lens before we call it done: a 2D animation that triggers whenever we tap. To do that we'll start by importing our animation sequence.

You can use the one I've created or make your own. We're going to import this a little differently than we do for regular image files, because we want Lens Studio to treat our image sequence as a single animation file instead of individual image files.

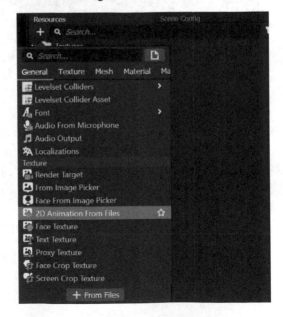

Select your image sequence files and hit Open. A box will appear that will give you lots of different options for how to customize your images into an animation. Since 2D animation files tend to be large files, compression settings can really come in handy for getting that fine balance of file size and what looks good. For our purposes, the default settings should be just fine. Click **OK**.

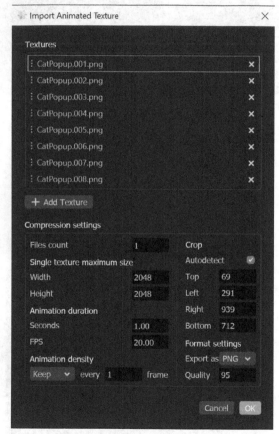

Select your newly created animation file and you can see it in action in the Inspector panel. Here you can see the file size and change its speed with the Duration or FPS boxes. You'll also notice an

"Always Play" checkbox, which loops our animation. We're going to leave that on for now so we can position our animation in the frame.

Rename your animation file to keep things organized. I'm calling mine "Cat animation."

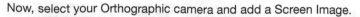

Now, select your Orthographic camera and add a Screen Image.

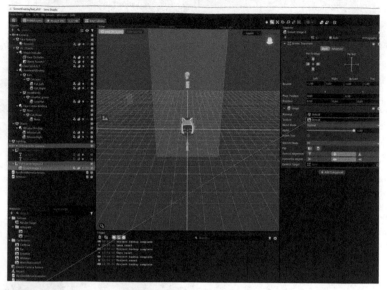

This will create a new Full Frame Region and a new Screen Image for your animation.

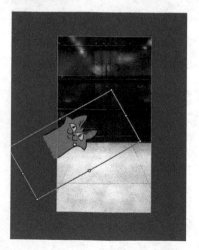

Drag your animation file into the texture of your new Screen image.

The animation will now be playing large in the preview window. Let's scale it down and position it off to the side of the screen in the 2D Scene Panel.

Texture			
Frames	20		
Frame Size	409x412		
RAM Usage	13164KB		
Total File Size	454KB		
Reverse	○	Ping Pong	○
Always Play	○		
Duration	1.00		
FPS	20.00		
Frame	—	Time	

Then we can go back to the Inspector panel options on the Cat animation (in the Resources panel) and switch Always Play to Off.

Let's add another copy of the Behavior script so we can trigger this animation with a tap. I've added one and renamed it "Trigger Anim Behavior."

Then change the Response Type to Animate Image and the animated Texture to Cat animation (or whatever you've named your animation file). Now when you tap, you'll trigger the cat animation.

And with that, the building phase of our amazing Lens experience is complete. Time to test, refine, and then publish! Congratulations!

Check out the section on the submission process for the final steps of publishing your Lens and getting your creation out there into the world.

PREVIEWING YOUR LENS IN SNAPCHAT

Once you've got your Lens how you want it, we'll want to make sure that it also looks good on our Snapchat as well. So, making sure your

Snapchat is paired to Lens Studio, hit the Send to Snapchat button.

Lens Studio will let you know it was successful.

Open your Snapchat and you'll be able to test it out. From here you can see a better representation of what the user will experience when they try your Lens. Move your head and change your expressions so you can make sure the placement of your objects are where you want them. Test out any of the scripting functionality as well, to make sure that is also working as expected. Remember that you can test your Lens anytime in the building process—the sooner you discover any problems with your Lens, the faster you can fix it and keep it from becoming a bigger problem down the road.

PROJECT 2:

3D WORLD SCENE—EGYPT DIORAMA

https://turnerbookstore.com/pages/lens-studio-projects

Estimated completion time: 3 hours

In Lesson 1, we learned how to modify a template, import assets, and the basics of building a face Lens. Now that you're a bit more comfortable with the process, let's step things up a bit by building a 3D world experience, which simply means using the device's back camera to place digital objects in the world on-screen. Scan this code with Snapchat and get a preview of what we're going to be building. In it, you will find a doorway to the pyramids of Egypt, with pop-up on-screen info when you point the camera at the targets. Step inside and be transported.

This Lens example demonstrates features that would be great for an educational exhibit, virtual gallery, or even a retail experience. I know it probably seems complicated, but it's totally something you can do and it's probably a lot easier than you might think.

3D ASSET PREPARATION

This Lens will be using a 3D scene that I created in Maya, so you won't need to create your own. I recommend following along with the art assets I've provided, unless you're experienced and comfortable with 3D software.

For those who are interested, here's a quick rundown of the important parts of its construction. Feel free to skip this subsection if you aren't interested—it's not crucial to the actual Lens experience build.

I first built the models of the key elements—Pyramids, Sphinx, monuments, portal, and wooden sign. Then I added the environment model, which is a large cube with a door cut in it (circled). And the Occluder, which is just a slightly larger version of the environment and is going to act as our Harry Potter invisibility cloak for everything we don't want to be seen.

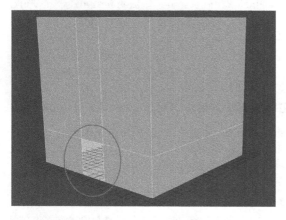

I assigned one material (Lambert) to all the main scene objects, and a separate material for the environment and Occluder.

UV LAYOUT

Next, I laid out the UVs for the objects. I'm using a single texture for all the main objects to economize file space, so I need to make sure none of their UVs overlap and that they're all oriented so I can easily texture them.

Animation

I've also added a bit of animation to the wooden sign, so you'll be able to see how animation works and how to use a Behavior script to control it. You will want to bake your animation keyframes if you're going to be using multiple animation layers. But it's not necessary if you just have a single animation.

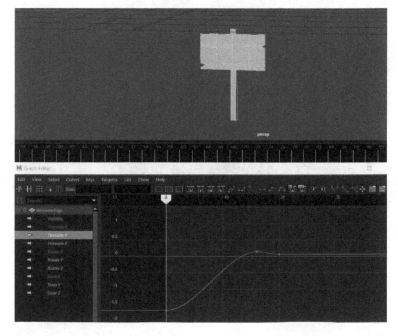

Exporting FBX

Lens Studio accepts FBX format for importing 3D models. The export guide available on their website does an excellent job of explaining how to do that.

https://lensstudio.snapchat.com/guides/3d/3d-object-export/

These are the settings I use:

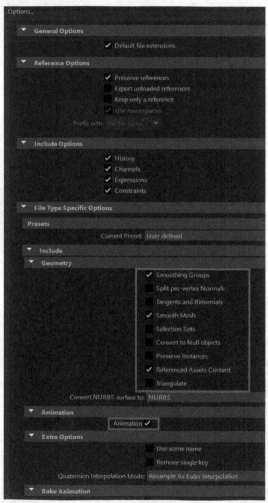

Note that if you have any animation you want to export with your FBX, you have to have the Animation box checked.

TEXTURING 3D

I've found that it's best to export a separate FBX of my scene that I use exclusively for texturing in Substance Painter—especially if there's an Occluder involved. Substance Painter lets you "bake" your mesh maps, which helps the program figure out the model's corners, grooves, and edges. These maps are essential for using its Smart Materials. Any unintended geometry collisions, intersections, or unnecessary geometry can make the texturing process more difficult. I find it's best to export and FBX with just the geometry I want to texture in it.

Here's what my textured model looks like in Substance Painter after I've textured it:

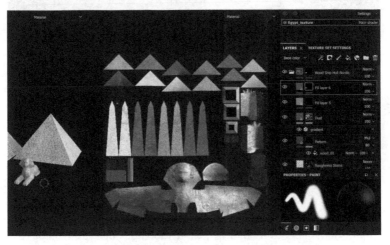

Substance Painter also has a Lens Studio export preset for exporting your final Color (base), Material Parameters, and Normal maps. (Remember that Lens Studio's preferred file formats are .PNG and .JPG.) Your resulting files will look like this:

Once you have your FBX files and textures created, you're ready to start building your Lens experience.

ASSEMBLING A 3D WORLD SCENE

Let's begin building this wonderful, educational Lens experience. Start by making sure you have all the art assets I've provided downloaded and available. Then start with a New Project and save it with an appropriate name.

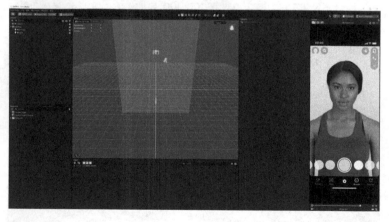

Next, let's Switch the Preview to the back camera, so we can properly see the experience we're building in a world environment. Remember that this is just a looping video that helps you see what you're building; it's possible to upload your own custom video if you like, but to really test your Lens you'll need to use the Send to Device button and test your Lens in Snapchat.

Then Import the Egypt Scene FBX by dragging the file into the Resources panel or clicking the + then, + From Files, also in Resources. When you import FBX files, they'll come with an additional options window. Default settings are what you'll typically use.

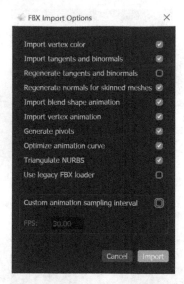

Then import our texture files found in the TX folder to our Resources panel as well.

I've immediately created a Textures folder so I can keep my project organized.

Let's go ahead and assign the imported texture files to their material. In the Egypt Scene FBX, go into the Materials folder and find the one called Egypt_texture and select it.

Jump over to the Inspector panel, and we'll find the places where we'll plug in our texture maps I created in Substance Painter. Click the checkbox and select the appropriate image map files from the Textures folder. I also like to make sure the underlying Base color is closer to white, so it doesn't make our texture maps look dull and dingy.

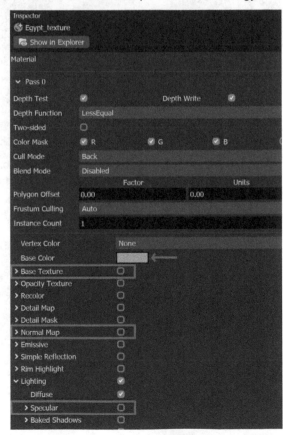

When you're done, it will look like this:

One quick final note: sometimes really complex Normal and Material Params maps will render in your scene with a lot of noisy artifacts. To smooth these out, hit the dropdown and select Mipmaps. Do this now for both the Normal and Material Params in the Egypt Scene.

You may have noticed that the FBX imported with a Environment_color.jpg file already applied to the Environment_tx material. How did that guy tag along for the ride? It was set to the Environment_tx material in Maya when I was creating the scene and it exported with the FBX. If for some reason the jpg didn't import (the background is just gray instead of a blue sky and sand), you'll have to manually import this file which can be found in the 2.1 Project -> Public folder and apply it to the Base Color of the Environment_tx Material using the same method we followed for the Egypt textures.

Our Egypt Scene is now set up and ready to be used in the objects panel. But before we pull it in, we need to prepare the scene so Lens Studio knows how to place our digital object in the real world on-screen.

To do that, we're going to use the World Object Controller. Let's add that now, in the Objects panel. It can be found under Helper Scripts.

You'll see that it imports with more than just a World Object Controller script itself. It comes with a Ground Grid, Touch Collision, and Matte Shadow objects—as well as the Red Panda FBX. We're going to delete the Red Panda momentarily, but you're probably wondering why it's displaying wrong. There's a couple of things we need to do to make the World Object Controller work properly.

Select the Camera in the Objects panel. Then in the Inspector panel, click + Add Component and select Device Tracking.

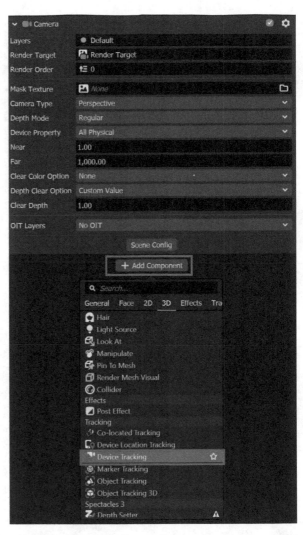

You can see that it's already looking better. But we need to also point the World Object Controller script to our newly created Device Tracking component.

Now the script is set up properly! You can use your mouse to drag the Red Panda around the scene and it stays along the ground plane in perspective of our video. Yay! This is fun.

Sorry, Red Panda, your time with us is done! Delete the Red Panda FBX from our Objects and Resources panels.

Our interactive controller is all set up and ready to receive our Egypt Scene object. Let's drag the Egypt Scene prefab in the Resources panel into the World Object Controller hierarchy.

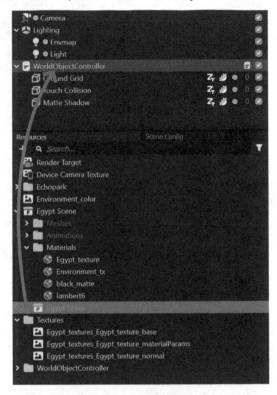

As you can see, the model is now in our scene, but you're probably saying, "What is this? An Egypt Diorama for ants?!"

It's tiny! No worries. We'll scale it up by going into the Inspector panel and changing the Scale to 42 and the Position Z to -420.00.

We can see that our Animation on the wooden sign is playing automatically. In the Animation Mixer, Uncheck the AutoPlay box so it stops. Let's also change the Cycles from -1 (cycle endlessly) to 1(cycle once).

Looking at our preview, you'll notice that we can see right through the back wall. That's because the Render Far distance on the Camera is cutting off at 1,000. Let's select the Camera and bump that up to 2,000.

Now our full model can be seen by the camera.

Let's change the color of our Occluder object so it actually masks out the geometry in the scene like it's supposed to. Go into the Resources panel, and under Materials, add a new Occluder material.

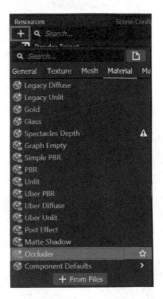

And selecting the Occluder object in the Objects panel, replace its existing material with the Occluder material.

With the Occluder in place, our Egypt Scene object becomes like our very own Tardis—it's bigger on the inside!

One final touch to add is the cool sci-fi material for the portal. To make that, we'll be selecting one of the very cool materials available in Lens Studio's Asset Library. Click the Asset Library button now.

Here you can find an amazing collection of assets, scripts, and effects to take your Lenses to the next level. There's new stuff here all the time, so it's definitely a resource you'll want to take advantage of.

Under the Materials tab, import the Hologram Material and close the Asset Library again.

Let's apply the Hologram material to the Portal object.

In the Preview panel, we can already see that the default settings will need to be adjusted. Let's select the Hologram material in the Resources panel, change the colors, tone down the glitch, and bump up the Scan Line density. Find the settings you think look best.

Now we have a proper portal to another world! Send it to your device and test it out. See if there's any tweaks you need to make before we move on to the next lesson.

If everything is working well, save it and version up!

ADDING INTERACTIVE INFO CARDS

With our Egypt Scene set up, now we can go about adding the handy information cards that pop up when we point the camera at them. Start by importing the PaperImg.png and Papyrus font, and—you guessed it—organizing them in our folders.

Create a Screen Image object just like we learned how to do in Lesson 1 and apply the PaperImg texture to it. In the Inspector panel, under Screen Transform, select the Fix Size option in the vertical direction. (This will allow us to properly move the card on-screen with a tween script. I'll explain more later.)

Now add two Screen Text objects nested under the Screen Image object hierarchy. Change the font to Papyrus, vertical alignment to Top, and color to black. Resize the text boxes on the two so they fit nicely to become a header and text body. Then change the Font Size on the first box to 40 and the second box to something smaller, like 22. If you followed all that, you'll have something that looks like this:

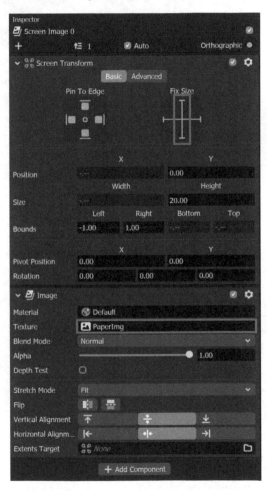

This first group will become our information for the Great Pyramid. Rename the Screen Image and text objects so we're not confused later when we're hooking up the scripts.

Let's fill in the information we want for that in the text box.

Title: **Great Pyramid of Giza**

Body: The *Great Pyramid of Giza is the oldest and largest of the pyramids in the Giza pyramid complex bordering present-day Giza in Greater Cairo, Egypt.*

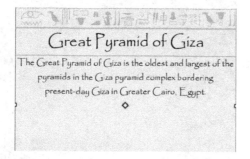

Duplicate the Pyramid Group and rename the objects to correspond with the Sphinx.

And change the text as well.

Title: **The Great Sphinx of Giza**

Body: *The Sphinx is a limestone statue of a reclining sphinx, a mythical creature with the head of a man and the body of a lion. Facing directly from west to east, it stands on the Giza Plateau on the west bank of the Nile in Giza, Egypt.*

We now have our information cards set up. We're now going to add motion tweens so our cards slide in with a bit of fun. In the Objects panel, add the Tween Manager from the Helper Scripts. It imports with a bunch of tween examples that are worth exploring how they work later.

Drag the Tween Manager script to the top of the hierarchy and delete the examples.

We're going to be moving the cards into view from off screen so to do that, they need to start off screen. Enable the Pyramid group (if it isn't already) and change its Screen Transform **Y Position to -15**.

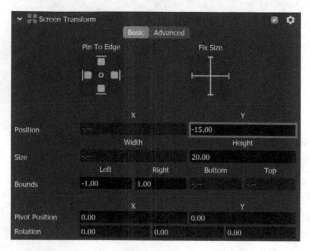

Then from the Resources panel in the Tween->Tween Types folder, we're going to drag **a Tween Screen Transform script** to the Pyramid Group in the Inspector panel.

NOTE: It's very important to use the Tween Screen Transform and not the Tween Transform script.

You'll see that this overrides our Screen Transform information. Here we give the tween a name ("Pgroup In"), change the start **position Y to -15**, and end **position Y to -7**. You can also play with the Easing Function presets to give the info card a jaunty bounce.

Since we don't want the card sticking around all the time after we've summoned it, we'll also need a tween to make it go away again. You can drag in a new Tween Screen Transform script or duplicate the one that we just set up with the Gear symbol [icon] and Copy + Paste.

On this one we'll name Pgroup Out and reverse the Start and End position values (-7 and -15 respectively). We'll also change the Time to be 0.2, so the Out tween goes faster than the In.

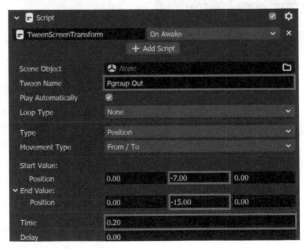

Now that we've seen the tween in action we can also switch OFF the Play Automatically checkboxes in both scripts. We're going to use a behavior script to trigger them.

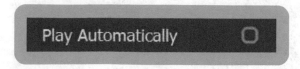

You now have your Tweens set up for the Pyramid group. I hope that was a fun process because you get to do it again for the Sphinx Group. Be sure and name your Tweens Sgroup In and Sgroup Out. This will be important when we set up the Behavior scripts!

We have one more thing to set up before going further: Focus targets! These will be what the user's camera has to point at before it triggers the info cards. The great thing is, we can use what's already available in Lens Studio to create these.

In the Objects panel, add a new Sphere from the Mesh menu.

Drag that sphere under the World Object Control hierarchy because we want it to move with exhibit. Also rename it "Pyramid target."

Then, hit the (W) key and use the move tool to position the sphere over in front of the Pyramid model. Let's also set the scale to 2.

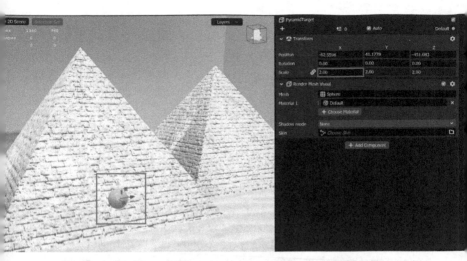

Duplicate the Pyramid Target sphere and rename it Sphinx Target. (You guessed it, we're going to position this one over by the Sphinx model.)

Now our targets are looking a bit boring. Let's jazz them up a bit with a hologram texture. Go into the Asset Library, import a new Hologram Material to your project, then apply it to your target spheres. If you did it correctly, they should look like this:

Now we're ready to set up a couple of Behavior scripts that will control the tweens using these target spheres. Add a new Behavior script to your Objects panel and name it PyramidController.

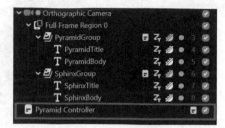

To set up this script, we're going to make the Trigger set to Looking At (meaning when one object is pointing toward another object within a certain number of degrees). Make the Looking Object our Main Camera (with the Device Tracking on it) and the Look Target is the Pyramid Target. Leave the Compare type as Is Less Than, and the Degrees to 10.00.

Now change the Response Type to Run Tween, the Target Object is PyramidGroup, and the tween name Pgroup In. (Be sure and match the tween name exactly the same as it is on your Tween Screen Transform script on the Pyramid Group.)

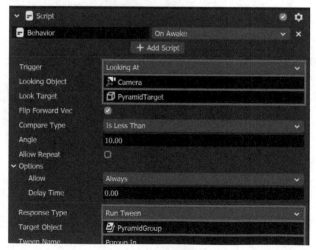

This will make our Info Card pop into view when the Pyramid Target is within a 10-degree viewing angle of the Camera.

Now all we have to do is change a couple of settings to make the card go away when the device is not pointed at the target. Copy and paste that same Behavior script right below on the same object. Change the Compare type to Is Greater Than, make the angle 10.1 (because we don't want the two scripts fighting each other at exactly 10), and finally change the Tween name to Pgroup Out.

We can quickly test to see if the script is working properly by grabbing the Pyramid Target object and using the Move Tool (W) to slide it left to right. If it is within the 10-degree viewing or "Looking At" angle, if our Pyramid Info card pops in and out like it should, then we know it's set up correctly.

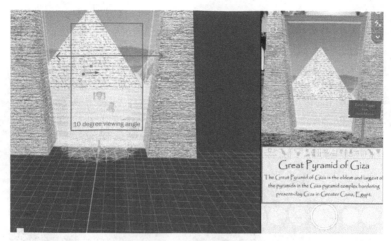

Great Pyramid of Giza

The Great Pyramid of Giza is the oldest and largest of the pyramids in the Giza pyramid complex bordering present-day Giza in Greater Cairo, Egypt.

We need the same scripts set up for the Sphinx, so we can just duplicate the Pyramid Controller and change its settings to correspond with the Sphinx Target and Sphinx Group.

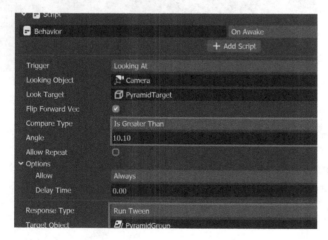

Again, quickly test by moving the Sphinx Target object into and out of view to make sure it's displaying and hiding the Sphinx Info Card correctly. This would also be a good time to send it to your device and make sure it's working properly there as well. If so, save and version up!

So now our Info cards pop up whenever we have the camera pointed at them, but that's actually a bit distracting. Let's set it up so this only happens when we're close to the targets.

Let's start by deactivating the Sphinx and Pyramid Controller scripts. Then add a new behavior script below them.

With this script we're going to use a Distance Check to make multiple things happen with one trigger. Let's go!

First, **rename the Behavior script to EnterTrigger**. Then set up the script with the following settings:

Trigger: Distance Check

Object A: Camera (the one with device tracking)

Object B: Portal object

Compare Type: Is Less Than

Distance: 160

Response Type: Send Custom Trigger

Trigger Name: Enter

What this Behavior script is doing is checking to see if the main camera is within 160 units of the Portal; if it is, the script will send out the custom trigger "Enter," so any other scripts listening for it will trigger.

Next, we'll create a pair of Behavior scripts (I've named them "ActivateControllers" in the object panel).

Set them up to be looking for the Custom Trigger "Enter," which will Enable the Pyramid and Sphinx Controllers objects.

Now when we test the Lens, you can see that the Info Cards activate only when we get close to the portal. This script will remain active once it's triggered, but you can always make another set of Behavior scripts that also deactivate the controllers again when the user moves away. I'll let you try that on your own for advanced practice.

If everything is working well, save, version up, and let's move on to the final part of this Lens experience.

Remember the wooden sign with animation that we switched off at the beginning of the tutorial? We're going to set it up so the sign animation triggers when the Lens experience starts.

Make a new text object under the Welcome Sign object.

You'll need to reposition the text object in front of the welcome sign with the Move tool.

Also adjust the font to Papyrus, font size to 8, and let's have a little fun with dynamic text for the message.

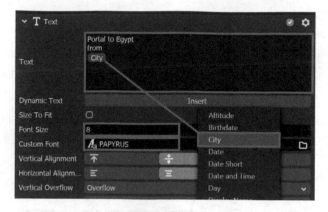

Now the sign will dynamically usher them from their current city to Egypt.

You'll notice an issue, however, when we created the text with our sign. They are no longer hidden by the Occluder. This can happen if you're messing with the hierarchy in a prefab. To fix this, all you need to do is drag the Occluder object to the top of the prefab hierarchy, like so:

The Text Object is still visible, so in the Inspector panel, check Depth Test to make it hidden by the Occluder as well.

All we need to do now is go back to the Animation Mixer on the Egypt Scene object and switch the AutoPlay On.

And with that, we've completed this 3D Portal to the Pyramids experience. Feel free to test it out and make tweaks and adjustments to fine-tune the interactive elements. This should demystify the process of using 3D models as well as adding interactivity with Behavior scripts.

PROJECT 3: IMAGE MARKER EXPERIENCE—VISIT MARS

https://turnerbookstore.com/pages/lens-studio-projects

Estimated completion time: 1.5 hours

In this lesson, we'll be tackling Image Markers, which is a really fun but very underused capability for AR experiences. It has some obvious limitations, the biggest being that the user must have the image in front of them to trigger the experience. To my mind, however, no other technology has the potential to disrupt the print industry more than augmented reality. Any movie poster, painting, magazine ad, or even book cover could be used to expand the message, heighten the experience, or provide information related to the print piece.

The work for an image marker begins way before we ever open Lens Studio. I would say the most critical element to your experience is the image itself that you'll be using for the marker. This will be what the computer vision will be looking for to initiate the Lens experience. Some images make way better image markers than others. By way of explanation, I like to use the metaphor of rock climbing. If you've ever done it, you know it's much easier to climb with lots of good grips to hold on to that have a large contrast with the wall. Image markers are like that too. You'll want to give the camera an image that it can easily "grab on to" and track. It's why QR codes are black and white with a unique arrangement of tiny squares. So, as you choose (or create) the image that you'll be using for the image marker, make sure it has good contrast and plenty of details for the camera to see. And another caution about the design itself is, don't make it too symmetrical or Snapchat might display your experience upside down or backward.

An experience consideration for making an image marker AR is to know how your image itself will be displayed. Will it be horizontal or vertical? Large or small? In good lighting or dimly lit? All these things can affect your overall presentation.

One final "best practices" item to consider is to incorporate the snapcode of your Lens into the design of the final print collateral. It's an easy visual clue that there's an AR experience that goes along with the image, and they have the code immediately accessible to scan it.

In this experience, I've created a retro poster to promote Mars tourism that comes to life with the Snapchat Lens.

Scan the snapcode below and aim your phone at the poster to trigger the experience.

Pretty fun, yeah? Of course, you'd never want to open a portal window to empty space like that in real life, but we can do all kinds of whimsical things in augmented reality. So let's get into building this thing!

For this experience, I built the 3D assets in Maya. The project models include the rocket ship, planet Mars, portal window, and space background. I also built a custom Occluder so we can make it look like the portal opens out into the scene.

I have two objects that I've animated in Maya: the rocket ship and the portal window. I've actually exported the portal window separately because we're going to be controlling that animation with a script later, so it's just easier to export them as separate FBX files and it saves us from a headache trying to control just the one animation later as we build the Lens. As you get more experienced building Lenses, you'll be able to anticipate problems and work around them.

QUICK AND DIRTY GUIDE TO TEXTURING IN SUBSTANCE PAINTER

I wanted to briefly sidebar into my process for how to create textures in Substance Painter. This isn't part of the main lesson, so if this isn't relevant, feel free to skip past this section. For anyone doing work in 3D, I cannot recommend it enough. It's second to none for making your models—and therefore your Lenses—look amazing. Now, just a caveat: There's a longer and more detailed (read: proper) way to create textures in Substance. They've got lots of tutorials and resources to teach you everything you could want to know. But that's not what this is. My process is about quickly getting that texture you need and getting back to building your Lens experience.

Much of the preparation for getting your model ready to texture will be done in your 3D program—clean geometry, orderly UV layout, and all the geometry with a texture/material applied to it. There's no right number of materials to use—typically, the fewer the better for file size considerations—but each texture map affords you greater details for the final look of your model. In this instance, we only need to texture one material, which covers the rocket and the metal of the portal window. And I've only exported an FBX for the part of the scene that we'll be needing for texturing in Substance Painter.

To get started, open Substance Painter, select File->New and use the Lens Studio template. Select the FBX that you've created just for texturing. And set the Document Resolution to 2048—which is on the high end of what a texture should be in Lens Studio, but we can always export at a lower resolution if we need to.

Then click OK and Substance will import your model.

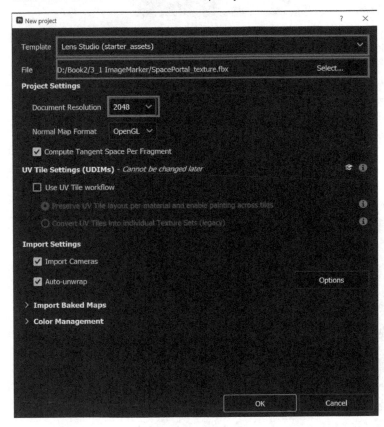

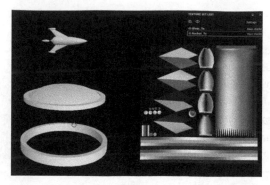

I like to check my model and its UV layouts before I go any further. I'm looking to make sure each element is a reasonable distance from the others so we don't get any weirdness when we bake the mesh maps. Also, go through the texture set list and check the UV maps are not overlapping each other. It's possible to update your 3D model after you have textures applied (Edit ->Project Configuration [select FBX]), but you may end up having to redo any hand-painted work, so it's best to start off with the most final version of your 3D model.

Now, go under Texture Set Settings and select Bake Mesh Maps. Baking is a process where the computer figures out what the effects of natural lighting will look like on your model and creates a series of maps, which helps our textures fake this effect (and saves us a typically processor-intensive endeavor).

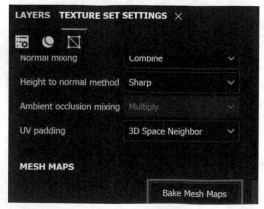

For Bake Settings, I make the output size 2048 and then hit the Bake Selected Textures button. You'll then see Substance go through and create the series of maps that will be used especially in Smart Materials.

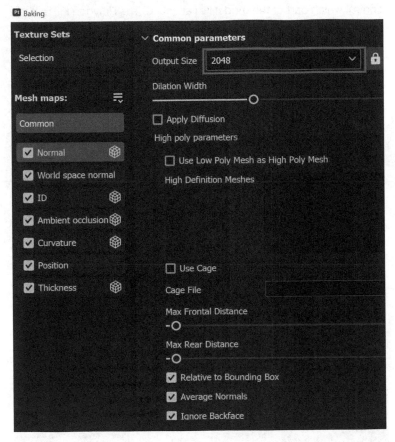

Now comes the fun part: making your model look pretty. Substance comes with a big library of available materials, Smart Materials, Smart Masks, brushes, and stencils. There's even more community-created materials available for download on https://share-legacy.substance3d. com/.

The core philosophy of making good materials is to start general and go specific—meaning work on the broad details first (base colors and procedurally generated materials) before you get into the fine brush work. I like to use folders and layer masks to stay organized and control which part of the model I'm affecting. The Polygon Fill tool is a lifesaver for quickly and cleanly masking layers for your model.

Another tip is that you can quickly toggle various parameters of a material or a fill that you're using with these buttons. If you only want to affect the color, for example, just deselect the height, rough, metal, nrm, and op.

Don't forget that there's a ton of tutorial videos from Adobe on YouTube (and other creators) that can help you way beyond what I'm covering here in this chapter (https://www.youtube.com/user/Allegorithmic).

Once you're done creating your textures it's time to export (File->Export Textures). Make sure you're using the Lens Studio output template, which will give you the Color, Normal, and Material Parameter maps. Here's where you can also choose a different file type or smaller size if you want. Hit the Export button and you're all set!

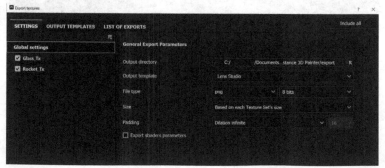

Again, this is my personal method for quickly creating texture maps for my 3D models. I'll include my Substance Painter project file with this lesson so if you're interested, you can open it up and see what I did.

BUILDING THE IMAGE MARKER EXPERIENCE

Even though we could start this project from scratch, there's a good template already available in Lens Studio, which has nearly everything we need set up already. So, let's open the Marker template and get it ready for our scene.

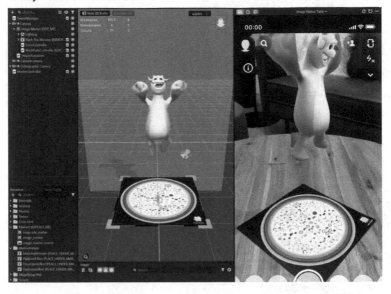

We can immediately delete the Mark the Monster [Remove Me] from the Objects panel.

Next, we see that Lens Studio's example uses the default image marker in the project and the preview, but for me, the best practice is to upload your own preview video and start with the final "Mars Poster" image marker. We do this so we don't have to tweak a bunch of settings down the line to make things look good on another marker.

To do this, you don't even need to print your image. Just pull up your poster image on your computer screen and record a quick video with Snapchat. Then email that video to yourself and upload in the Preview panel with the + From Files button.

Your video will show up at the top of the list of previews under My Files. I've provided the example video that I recorded in the project files: MarsPreview1.MP4. Import and select it now.

We can see that the Lens is now looking for the default image marker and not finding it in our new preview.

Let's add our new Image Marker image. This won't be like importing a regular image (by the + From Files button). We need to go to the Resources panel, select +, and then choose the Image Marker asset. It will then prompt us to pick the image we're using for the image marker. Select the file MarsPoster_color.jpg from our asset files. Lens Studio will import it specifically as an image marker file.

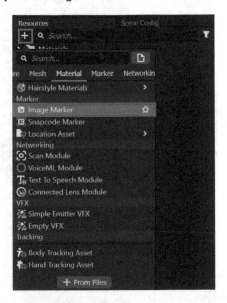

Select the Image Marker Tracking object in our Objects panel and change the Marker to our own MarsPoster_color.

We also need to update the preview image. Drag the MarsPoster_color.jpg into the Resources panel. Then select the Magnifying Hint Script under the Orthographic Camera. Make the Preview Texture our newly imported MarsPoster_color texture.

Then we'll import our own FBX (SpacePortal_Scene, SpacePortal_Door) and Image files (Glass Opacity, Stars, Meteor) from our Assets and arrange them all in our own folders.

In the Objects panel, we can delete the Helper Functions Script and Capture Camera—these are used for the ground bounce effect for Mark and we no longer need them.

Since we've got two model files that we're using we want them to stay together. Let's create an empty Scene Object under the image

marker and name it MarsGroup. Then we'll add the SpacePortal_
Scene and SpacePortal_Door prefabs under that. (Remember that the
Prefab is the part of the FBX file that has the icon with the little 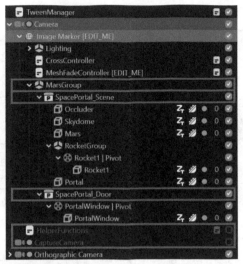 in
it.)

With our 3D files in the scene, we see that we immediately have an
issue. Our objects are rotated -90 degrees. All we need to do to fix it
is compensate with a 90-degree X rotation on the Mars Group object.
We can also use this opportunity to fine-tune the position of the models in relation to the image marker. Position X to 0.07, Y to 0.2, and the
Scale to 0.68.

Before we go any further, let's apply our awesome textures we created
in Substance Painter to our materials. In the Resources panel, find
the SpacePortal_Scene object and select the Rocket_tx material and
apply the base, normal, and material parameters files for it.

Even though both our FBX's import with a "Rocket_tx" material, they're each using their own. We simply apply the material from the SpacePortal_Scene to the door so they're both matching. Select the PortalWindow in the Objects panel and drag the updated Rocket_Tx to replace the previous one.

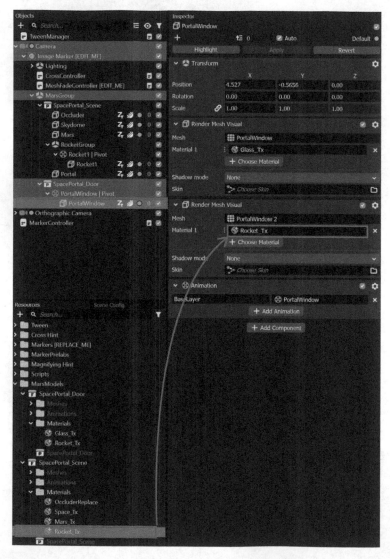

Lens Studio used to include a nice default glass material we could easily add to use for the portal window. Fortunately, I've saved a copy that we can now import in the Resources panel using the + From Files button and selecting the Glass_mat.lsmat file in the provided assets. Import it now.

Again, select the PortalWindow object and this time replace the Glass_Tx material with the Glass material that we just modified.

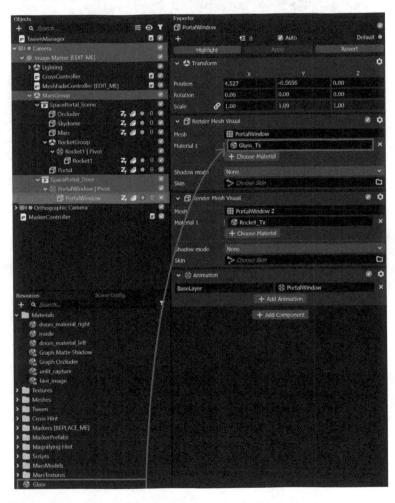

Let's also do the same thing for our Occluder object, replacing it with the Graph Occluder material already in the file's Materials folder located in the Resources panel.

Note: Lens Studio recently updated the Graph Occluder material to just calling it Occluder material. Just know that they're the same thing.

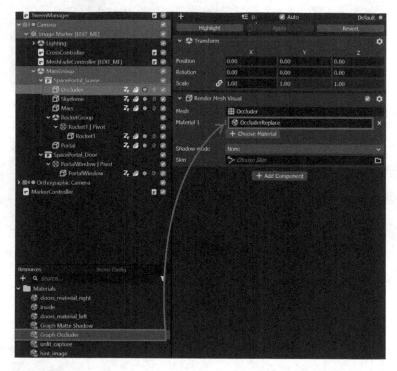

Let's do one final aesthetic tweak to our Mars_Tx material found in the SpacePortal_Scene model. Select the material and check the Rim Highlight box. Change the color to hex code #ff5500 (deep orange). Change the Intensity to 0.8 and the Exponent to 1.7. This is going to give our planet Mars model a nice glow effect on the edges. I frequently use the Rim Highlight on materials to improve the overall look to a model.

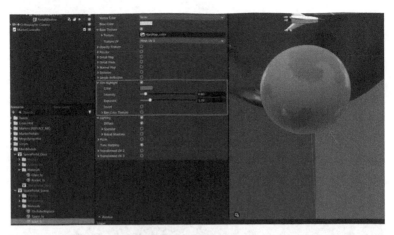

You'll notice that our planet Mars isn't rotating. Let's fix that with a Tween script. You'll see that our project already has a Tween Manager, so no need to add a new one. All we have to do is select our Mars object in the Objects panel and add on a TweenTransform script from the Resources panel Tween-TweenTypes folder. Select the Mars Object and drag the TweenTransform script into its Inspector panel.

Here are the settings I changed on the TweenTransform:

Loop Type: Loop

Type: Rotate

Movement Type: Offset

Offset: 90 (z-axis)

Additive: ☑

Time: 5.00

Easing Function: Linear

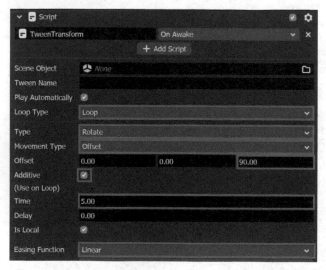

That gives our planet Mars a nice continuous rotation.

We have two more elements to add to this experience to finish up the look of this Lens: the stars and the meteor. To do that, we'll build from the skills we learned in earlier lessons.

Create a new image object under the Image Marker object hierarchy and name it Stars.

Select the Stars object and apply the Stars texture to it. Make the scale 15. Also change the Blend Mode to Add, so our stars show up a bit brighter.

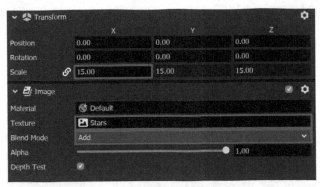

Let's set the stars in motion with a Tween. Add a TweenTransform to our Stars object.

Set the following options.
Loop Type: Loop
Start X, Y, Z: 5.00, 3.00, -2.00
End X, Y, Z: -5.00, -3.00, -2.00
Time: 0.4
Ending Function: Linear

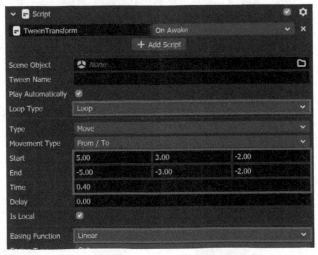

To add the Meteor, all we have to do is duplicate the Stars object, rename it Meteor, and adjust a few settings.

Replace the Stars with the Meteor texture. Change the X value start and end to 10 and -10, and add a delay of 4.0.

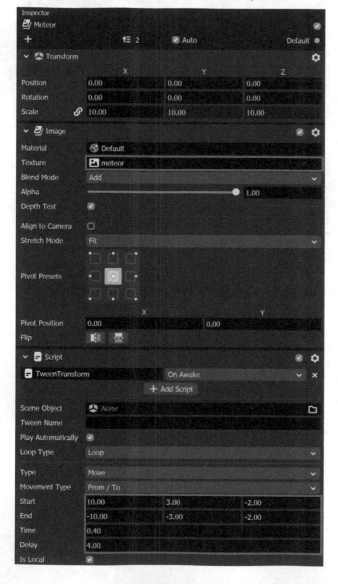

Finally, let's stop the animation cycle on the portal window—we're going to be controlling that with a script in the next section.

Select the SpacePortal_Door object, uncheck AutoPlay and set the cycles to 1.

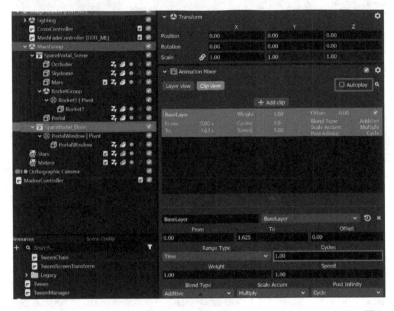

Our scene is now set up and we're ready to add the interactivity. This is a great place to save our project and version up.

3D ANIMATION WITH INTERACTIVE TRIGGERS

In this part of the lesson, we're going to set up the interactivity to open and close the portal with a tap. We can accomplish this with a couple of Behavior scripts, of course!

First, add a Behavior script and name it OpenControl. (See Chapter 1.3 for a refresher on Behavior script setup if you need it.) Set the Trigger to On Custom Trigger and set the Trigger Name to Open. Response type is Animate Mesh; select the Animation Mixer for Space-Portal_Door, and the Layer name is BaseLayer (make sure you match it exactly).

We can use this script and modify it for the trigger to close the portal animation. Duplicate the OpenControl Behavior script and rename it CloseControl.

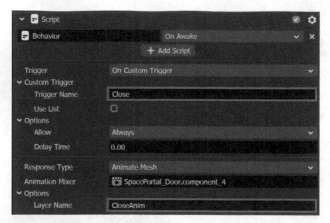

Change the Trigger Name to Close and the Layer Name to CloseAnim. These open and close our portal window, but we need another script that tells it what action to perform.

Let's add one more Behavior script and call it BehaviorControl. Make the Response Type Send Custom Trigger, check the Next In List box, and add values for Open and Close. This allows us to toggle between the Open and Close animations.

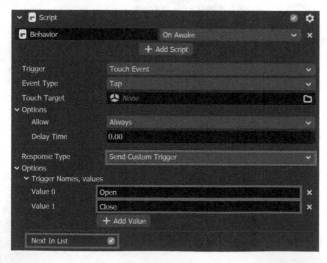

Let's jump back to our Space Portal Animation mixer. If we select it, we'll see that we have an animation clip called BaseLayer, which opens the portal window. But you'll notice that we don't actually have an animation clip to close it. Since we're clever, we can build it from our base layer clip!

Hit the + Add Clip button. Name it CloseAnim and hit the Reverse button. Change the Range Type to Frames. Now in the From and To for the range, make the clip go to 36 frames. Finally make the Cycles 1.0. Now we've got our Close portal animation!

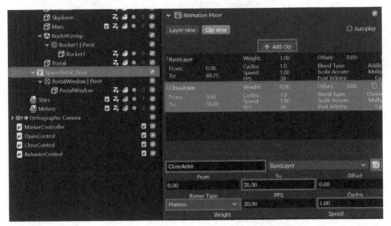

With that, our interactive portal open and close should work! Look at your preview window to make sure it is in fact working. Note that clicking in the preview window may actually reset your Lens, so to actually test the interactivity, you'll have to send the Lens to Snapchat and test it in the real world. (You can just pull up the jpg marker image of the Mars poster on your computer screen if you don't want to print it off.)

Let's add one more thing to this Lens, so our users know that we worked so hard to add that interactive element—a screen hint.

Let's add another Behavior script onto our Behavior Control script. Make the Trigger a Marker Tracking Event—the Event Type will be Marker Found—and select the Image Marker from our scene. Let's only allow this Once, since the user will get the idea. And the Response Type will be to Show Hint. Our Hint will be TAP!

Now when Snapchat detects our image marker, it will give the Snap-chatter a single hint to tap on the window to open it.

And with that, our Visit Mars image marker experience is complete!

3D CHARACTER—PENCIL GUY

https://turnerbookstore.com/pages/lens-studio-projects

Estimated completion time: 2 hours

I'm really excited to teach you how to build this next Lens. It's a style of Lens that I've developed over time and has become far and away my most popular. If you've ever used the Potato Lens, this will be very familiar. Here's what we're going to be creating.

There's a fair bit of complexity to this Lens, but when you're done you'll know more about chain physics, face blend shapes, and how to add a green screen effect behind your character. Let's get started.

3D MODEL SETUP FOR CHARACTERS

Much of the success of this type of Lens depends on how you build it. Here's how I go about creating and setting up my characters in Maya so they'll work well in Lens Studio.

I start with an appealing character design. This one uses a lot of basic primitive shapes for its construction. You can see in the wireframe view that we have plenty of polygons for the shape. If you have too few polygons, our character will look blocky and too many will have a negative effect on our Lens performance.

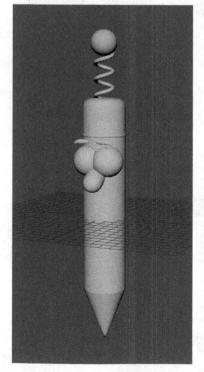 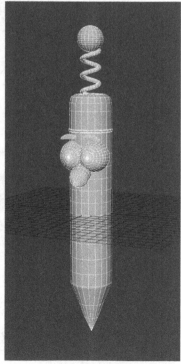

I've assigned Materials to the geometry. In this case, I've given the main pencil body one material, the eyes/nose/eyebrows/topper another material, and one more material for the fuzzy ball on top (which we're going to be swapping with a great material from the asset library).

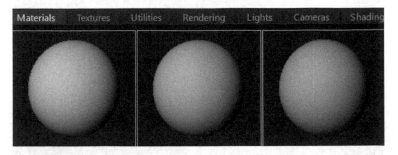

We'll make sure our geometry's UV layout for each of the materials is clean as well. Like I mentioned in earlier lessons, having proper UV layout is the basis for good-looking textures.

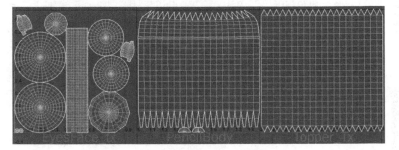

After you're happy with your UV layout and before you go any further, in Maya at least, it's good to delete history on your geometry. If you don't, it can create all kinds of weird problems when you're trying to use the model in Lens Studio.

Next, I've set up a Head Joint (joints are sometimes called bones in other programs) and a Body Joint. The head joint will end up tracking with the center of the user's face in the Lens. The body will have a script applied that makes it follow the head joint with a delay, which gives our character its fun movement.

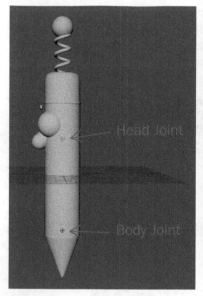 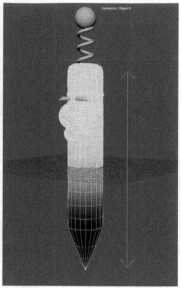

Next, we'll "skin" the geometry to the joints. This process assigns the geometry to move with a single or multiple joints. We'll want to check (and often adjust) the skin weights with the weight painting toolset. I look for a smooth and uniform transition from light to dark. This ensures our character's movement will look more natural and keep its shape/volume as the Snapchatter moves in the Lens. You can actually test the motion by moving the head or body joint around inside your 3D program (just make sure you return the joint to its original position).

For the Topper geometry, I know we're going to be using chain physics, so we'll want to have a joint chain ready for that. I skinned the topper geometry separately just to that topper joint chain so it's much easier to control the skin weights. I then assigned the chain to be children of the Head Joint, so it will move right along with that.

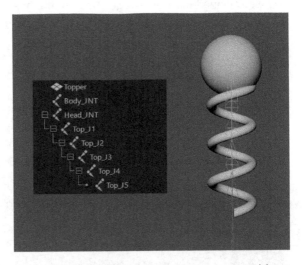

I created this character with Blend Shape eyebrows so you could see how the process of setting up expression-driven blend shapes in Lens Studio works. For blend shapes, you're starting with your original geometry and creating versions of it in different shapes, which the program will morph from one position to another. There are great videos on YouTube that can teach you exactly how to make blend shapes for the 3D software that you're using. I've created one for each of the five main eyebrow positions found in the script we will be using. You'll notice that I've named each piece of geometry following the naming convention used in the script as well. That way, when we get the script hooked up, the blend shapes start working immediately. You'll see what I mean when we get to that in the Lens build.

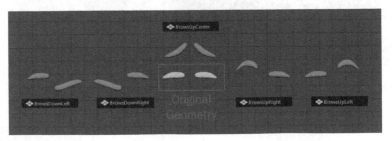

I've also skinned the eyebrow geometry to the head joint. It's important to do this after you've made the blend shapes or you'll get some weird deformations going on. And remember that you don't need to export the individual blend shape geometry when you're creating the FBX. You only need the main object that has the blend shape node applied to it.

We're now ready to export our FBX and create our textures in Substance Painter (see Lesson 3 for more about Substance Painter).

BUILDING THE 3D CHARACTER LENS

Let's start building this Lens with a fresh project in Lens Studio. In the Resources panel, import and organize the assets that I've provided.

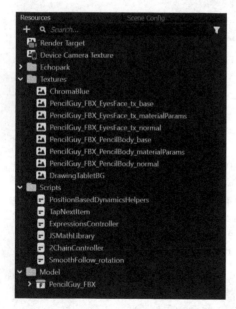

Next go into our FBX and assign the Base, Normal, and Material Params texture files to the PencilBody and EyesFace_tx. Don't forget to adjust the Base Color to near white #e7e7e7 if your base color is dark gray. Lesson 2 has a refresher on this process if you need one.

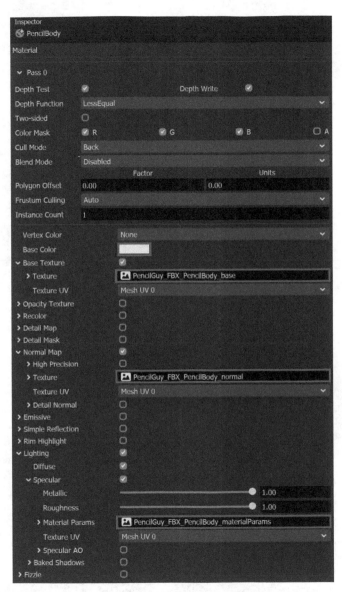

In the Objects panel, create a new Head Binding and delete the Face
Occluder that comes with it.

Drag the PencilGuy_FBX prefab under the Head Binding hierarchy.

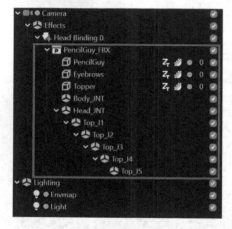

Let's quickly take care of the fuzzy pom on the pencil topper before we go any further. In the Assets Library, add the Material called Mane Fur created by the incredible Max van Leeuwen (Snapchat: @maxeflats).

Assign the Mane Fur material to the topper by swapping it for the Topper_Tx on the Topper object. Feel free to jump into the Mane Fur material's settings and customize it however you think looks best.

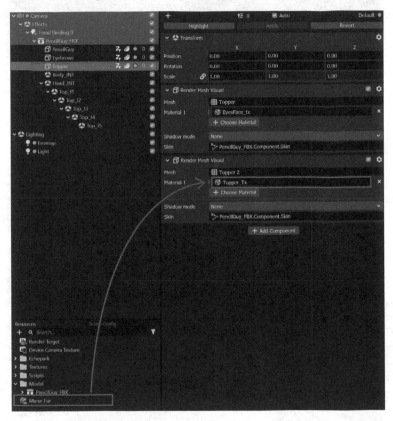

Our model is now looking good. But if we look in the Scene panel, we see that our model is a bit small and it's not quite where it needs to be in order to move well with the face. Let's fix that now with our Move Tool and Scale settings on the PencilGuy_FBX prefab. I set the Scale to 1.6 and I like to align the model's eyes with the Head Binding eye position. It has the best "feel" for the user as they move in the Lens.

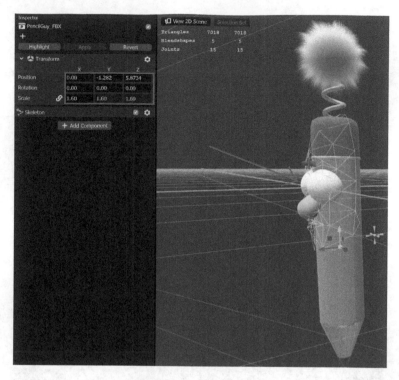

Let's add the Snapchatter's eyes and mouth to this. Create a new Face Inset and reparent it to the Head Binding 0. Then delete the Face Inset Binding—we don't need it.

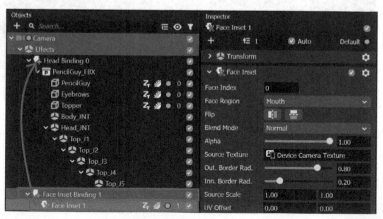

Rename the Inset to Mouth and adjust the Outer Border Radius to 0.2 in the Inspector panel so we get a tighter edge around the mouth inset.

Duplicate the Mouth Inset twice and change the names to Left Eye and Right Eye. Then for each one, change the Face Region to the corresponding left and right eye.

In the 3D scene view, adjust the size and position of the Mouth and Eye Insets. I like to scale up the eyes, which gives the character a cute, cartoony, and expressive face. Remember to check from the side view to make sure the insets aren't floating out in front of the model.

Let's now give the Pencil Guy the fun body movement that these Lenses are known for. Select the Body_JNT and add a Child Scene Object.

Rename it Body Follow. This is going to create a locator in the exact spot of our body joint. We do this because we want to track that spot where the body joint will then follow in relation to the head joint. This is a quick and easy way to do that.

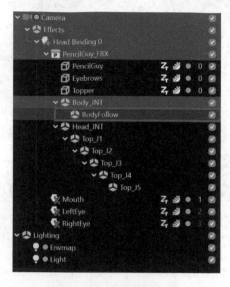

Now reparent that Body Follow object to the Head_JNT.

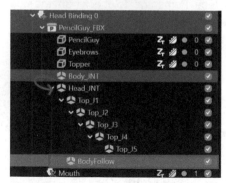

Then drag the Body_JNT outside of the Head Binding hierarchy so it isn't tracking with it anymore.

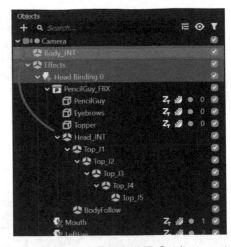

Add the SmoothFollow_rotation script to the Body_JNT. Set its target the BodyFollow object and set the Smooth Speed and Rot Smooth Speed both to 0.3.

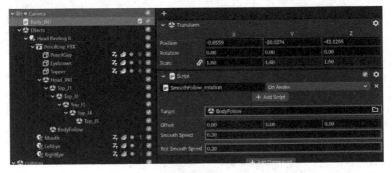

Now we see the body joint tracking along smoothly (with a slight delay). Cool!

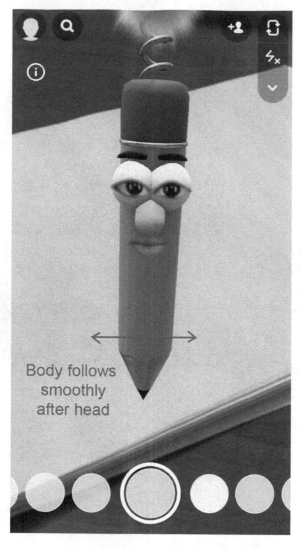

Let's add the background image next.

Add a new **Screen Image**. That will give us the Orthographic Camera, Full Frame Region, and the Image object.

Rename the Image to Background. Assign it the DrawingTableBG file and change the stretch mode to Fill and Cut (so our background looks nice when someone uses this Lens on Snap Camera).

As you can see (or not see), our background image is in front of our Pencil Guy character. That's easy to fix.

Go to the Scene Config panel (right beside the Resources panel) and swap the order of the Orthographic Camera and the perspective Camera (it's just called Camera).

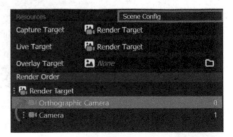

Let's now add the Chroma key background effect—in consideration of the Twitch streamers who love using these types of Lenses.

Duplicate the Background Image object. Rename it Chroma and assign its texture as the ChromaBlue file. (We're using chroma blue in this case because our Pencil Guy has a green nose and we want to give the video software a nice solid, different color to grab and make invisible.)

Add the TapNextItem script to the Object panel (I've renamed it NextItem) and the Background and Chroma image objects to its values. Unlike the Behavior script that makes us choose which action makes it work and what we want it to do, the TapNextItem script does one thing—select the next item in the list—so there's no further options for this script.

Now when you tap, it will switch between the background images. You can even add more if you want so it can switch between a bunch of different backgrounds.

We could call this Lens done at this point but I've added a couple of bonuses to teach you a couple of other functions that can be great for these types of Lenses.

ACTIVATING CHAIN PHYSICS

We already have a nice joint chain rigged up on the top of Pencil Guy's head. Let's make it move around with fun physics.

First, there's a couple of scripts we need to set up to make physics work in our scene. At the top of our Objects panel add the JSMath-Library and PositionBasedDynamicsHelpers. I named this script group Physics Scripts. In the JSMathLibrary script, check the Settings box and Add All. If you don't do this, Physics won't work in your scene.

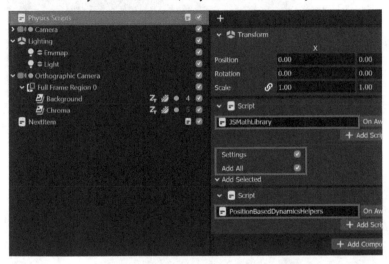

Now we can go to the Head_JNT and add the 2ChainController script. Add the Joints down the chain in order (it matters!) and check the Add Rotation box. Change the Force to 0.4 in the Y direction. There's lots of fun tweaks and settings you can play with to get your physics looking the way you want. Changed Iterations to 2, just so the movement is a touch smoother.

There you go! Physics!

DRIVE BLEND SHAPES WITH EXPRESSION CONTROLLER

You can actually create an entire 3D character whose expressions, mouth movements, blinks, and everything are driven by Blend Shapes. In this lesson, I'll get you started by showing you how to hook up this character's eyebrows.

It's important to note that the FBX that you're trying to set this up for must already have blend shapes built for it. You can quickly check if the object has been imported with blend shapes by clicking on the object in the hierarchy, and you should see the blend shape sliders.

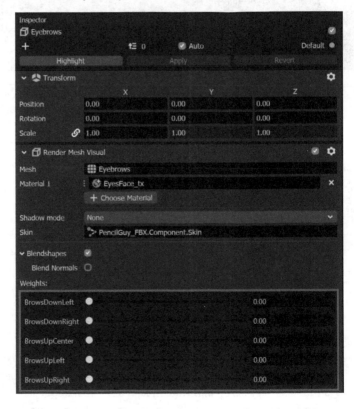

You can even move the sliders and see them in action in the Scene panel.

One thing the expression controller needs to work is a Face Mesh object. Start by adding a Face Mesh object to our scene now.

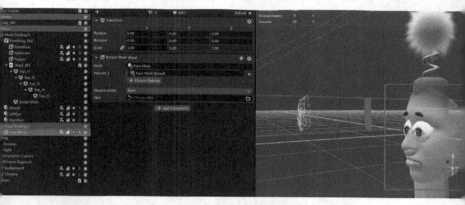

Now we need the mesh, but we don't want to see it. Let's create a special material for it. Create a new Unlit Material and rename it "Invisible."

Then Uncheck the Depth Test, Depth Write, and the Color Mask R, G, and B boxes.

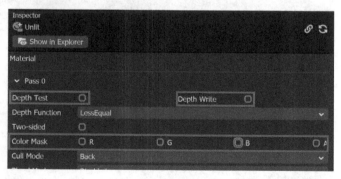

Select the Face Mesh and assign it with the Invisible Material. Now our face mesh is still in the scene but it doesn't show up. All we need from it is the face expression information it will be providing.

Select the PencilGuy_FBX prefab and add the Expression Controller script to it. It's best practice to put the Expression Controller on the Prefab, so it's easy to find it if you need to jump back in and make adjustments. Select the Eyebrows.Render Mesh Visual for the Blend Shape Component. Check the Advanced box and assign the Face Mesh to the one we just created.

And with that our Blend Shapes are working! Test them with one of the Raise Eyebrows videos in the Preview panel, or try them yourself by sending the Lens to your Snapchat.

TROUBLESHOOTING BLEND SHAPE EXPRESSIONS

It happens to the best of us sometimes. We create some awesome blend shapes and after we hook up the expression controller, nothing happens. After double-checking that we assigned the expression controller to the right object, and checked the object itself to make sure that it actually did import with blend shapes, there's one more place to check.

Check the Custom Expressions box and go into the face part that you've got blend shapes for. You'll see the different expressions that drive the blend shapes. Check the Blend Shape names here in the script and make sure they match the Blend Shape names you have assigned to your object. This is the main culprit of why my blend

shapes sometimes don't work. I've named them wrong. Just change
the names here to match what you called them and everything should

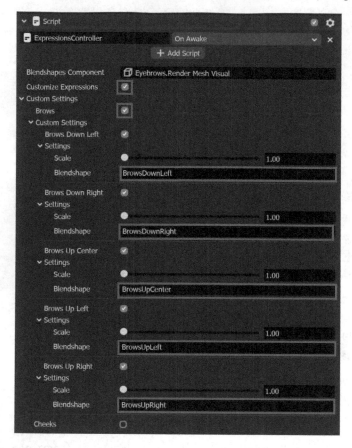

start working again.

And here you'll also find an added bonus! You can bump up the scale
factor if you're finding that the expressions are too understated. Crank
up the multiplier and then a little will go a long way!

And with that, our 3D character Pencil Guy is complete! Now you
can do everything that I can with these Lenses. Use this power re-
sponsibly!

3D BODY TRACKING—LASER VIKING

https://turnerbookstore.com/pages/lens-studio-projects

Digital fashion is quickly becoming popular with designers and retailers alike. It lets the customers try on augmented reality versions of everything from clothes, shoes, hats, watches—pretty much anything you can think of. This leads to higher customer satisfaction and fewer returns. And there's even some fashion you can buy that only comes in digital versions. It's certainly worth exploring the possibilities of what this new technology can do and how you can use it. Let's create our own digital fashion with a 3D body tracking Lens.

The major portion of the work for these types of Lenses will be done in your 3D modeling software. You can create with basic geometry or use the cloth simulation to help you make even more realistic-looking folds for your garments. There's even a program called Marvelous Designer, which is specifically designed to help you create awesome-looking 3D clothing.

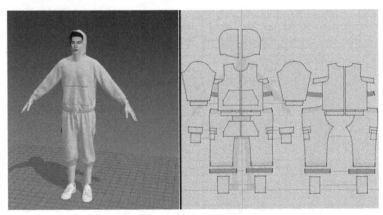

I'm going to show you the basics on how to get your 3D model to move with the body tracking rig. We start with the blank body model available in Lens Studio. This not only gives us the scale and dimensions needed for our own geometry, but it comes with a handy rig that's set up and everything's already named correctly. Don't redo work that you don't have to!

Now we can go about building our own digital fashion piece that's sure to turn heads in Paris and Milan. Here's my concept art for this masterpiece. I call it Laser Viking. It's really a statement piece for that time-traveling marauder on the go.

Let's get to work building the geometry, assigning materials, and laying out the UVs.

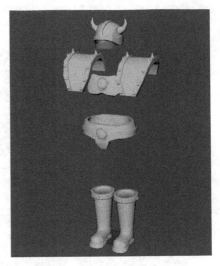

Then we take it into Substance Painter and make it look pretty. Remember that a good model tells a story—your texture is a big part of that. In this case, our armor has seen more than its share of action, so let's make it look banged up.

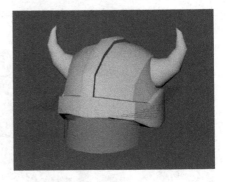

We'll jump back into our 3D software and set up the rig. This may be the most important step. If your model isn't set up to move well with the body, it'll break the illusion.

I'm skinning the model parts to the corresponding joints on the rig. Since they're supposed to be bulky pieces of metal, we don't have to worry so much about bends. Chest, shoulders, hips, and feet/legs all get their own piece.

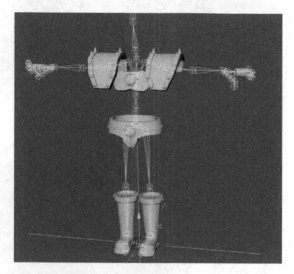

The one exception to this is our helmet. We're actually going to use a Head Binding in Snapchat for that, so we won't skin the helmet to the body rig. We will set the helmet's position to 0,0,0 and export it with our FBX.

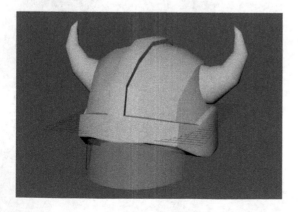

Now we'll export everything (including the reference geometry) as one FBX.

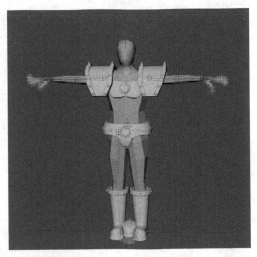

Now we're ready to open Lens Studio. Even though there is already a Body Mesh Template (that I definitely recommend you check out), we're starting with a new scene so I can show you just how easy it is to set up 3D body tracking.

Import the FBX and image assets. Let's also change our preview to the Body video.

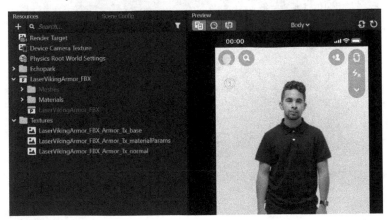

Now we can assign our textures to the Amor_tx material.

In our Object panel, let's add a Full Body Tracking system.

Then add the LaserVikingArmor prefab below it in the hierarchy. We can see in the preview that the model is moving with the body, but it's not right yet.

Select our 3D Body Tracking object and look at its Inspector panel. Here we find slots for all the different joints that the tracking object is controlling. Wow! There's sure a lot of them and we could certainly go through and plug in each one, but I'm lazy, so let's do it the easy way. Just hit the Match Hierarchy button.

Because we used the example rig body, all we have to do is choose the root joint in the rig (called dBody_Rig: Skeleton in this case) and the script will zoom through the rig and plug all the values in for us! Awesome!

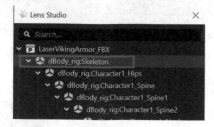

Check it out in the preview panel—our rig is moving right with the person's body now. How cool is that?

Let's now use that gray bodysuit geometry as our Occluder. Create a
new Occluder material in the Resources panel. Select the four geometry parts of the suit in the Objects panel (called head_low, hand_L_low,
hand_R_low, and body_low). Then drag the Occluder material into the
Material 1 slot in the Inspector panel.

Now our brave Laser Viking looks like he's actually wearing that armor.
Pretty nice!

But that helmet is still down at his feet. Let's get it on his head.
Let's do this by creating a new Head Binding in the Objects panel.
Then reparent the Helmet object to the Head Binding.

Before we go further. Since we're working with Occluders, we can actually make them visible to us without making them visible in the Lens itself. In the Scene panel, click the gear in the upper right corner, select Occluder Visualization, and then Visualize.

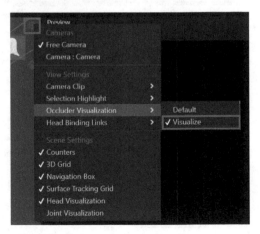

Now we can move the helmet model up into position on the Head Binding and see exactly where it should be positioned.

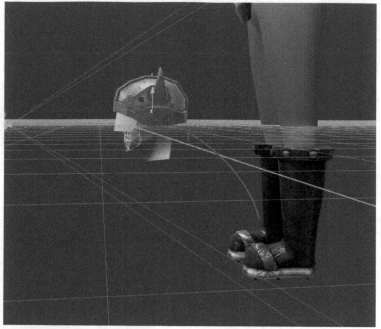

When we look at the preview, we see that the helmet is now tracking with the head, but I can see that we've got a problem. The Occluder from the body rig is putting a hole in our helmet.

No worries! Let's go back to the Object's panel and deactivate the Head_low Occluder object.

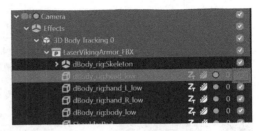

We've got a visor that's got a pretty plain texture right now. Let's jump into the Asset Library and import the Soap Bubble material.

Then Select the Helmet geometry in the Objects panel and drag to replace the Visor_Tx with our Soap Bubble Material.

Now our suit works for the first person it detects, but what if we want the same setup to work for additional users? Easy enough. Let's start by duplicating the hierarchies for the 3D body tracking and head binding objects.

Then change both the face and object index on the newly duplicated objects to 1. That makes our armor and helmet look for the second person on-screen.

We can keep doing this for additional characters by duplicating and changing the index. We can even customize the models for other characters, so they're not all the same.

And there you have it! A 3D body-tracked outfit that looks amazing. Our Laser Viking is ready to do mighty battle on the moonbase of Titan or slay on the catwalks of New York Fashion Week.

Remember to save your progress and test it out!

Now that you've built all these awesome Lenses, let's run through how you get them uploaded and out to the Snapchat world. This process begins with first checking the Logger to make sure that our Lens doesn't have any errors, broken scripts, or any other problems that will cause it to get rejected in Review.

Then make sure our Project File Size is accurate. Lens Studio will give you a quick glance at your utilization and whether it exceeds the allocated amount. Just because your project is getting toward the upper limit doesn't mean you can't publish it, but optimizing can really help make your overall experience better for the Snapchatter.

Quick Tip for Optimizing

If you see that your Lens project needs to go on a diet, there's a quick way to help it slim down. In my experience, the files that take up the most space in your project with be image files. PNGs tend to be worse offenders than JPEG, which is why I'm partial to using the latter (especially when I'm exporting a set of 2k textures from Substance Painter).

The good news is that Lens Studio has a built-in image optimization feature. Select the image in the Resources panel, and the Inspector panel will give you some options for optimization.

You can optimize for performance or size, with further settings for a low, medium, or high quality. Remember that we're going for the best balance between good quality and performance with our experience, so experiment and see what works best for you.

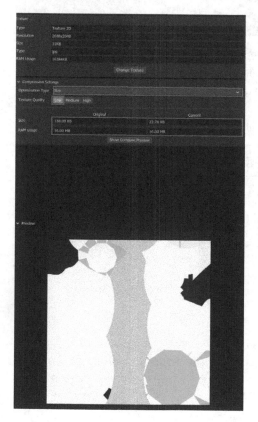

Let's jump into the Project Info window and set up the Lens name, icon, and preview.

Give your Lens a memorable name that people will be able to easily find with a search. I recommend against unconventional spellings or something that doesn't correspond to the experience.

Under "This Lens is Made for" is an option that helps Snapchat know where to serve your Lens experience. Best practice is only to check the box(es) that pertain to how people will be using your Lens. If it's for the user's face, it's for the front camera. If you've made a world experience, it's for rear camera. And Spectacles are their own unique thing. Don't check Front and Rear cameras if you don't have an experience created for both.

The hint is something you can add here that will give the Snapchatter a quick suggestion on how to trigger an interactive element when the lens first starts. There's a long list of possible hints, which can give you an idea of what interactive triggers you might try in a future Lens.

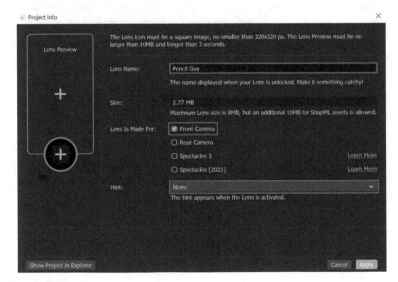

Let's add our Lens icon next.

The icon might be the first thing a Snapchatter sees about your Lens, so it's good to have an appealing one that makes a person stop and want to try your experience out. Little or no effort put into creating the icon doesn't bode well for the quality of the experience. Does it have to be a work of art? No, but here are my three guidelines for creating good icons:

1. Looks good at large and small size
2. Not overly busy or complicated
3. Using color, shape, and space to communicate your idea

I've created this icon for my Pencil Guy Lens, which hopefully looks fun and appealing, inviting the user to try it. I like using gradient backgrounds with a simple character representation rather than an actual screenshot of my Lens, which could be hard to recognize once the icon is displayed in the Lens Carousel of Snapchat.

Lens Studio prefers a 320x320 PNG for the icon file. More details and icon template files for Photoshop and Illustrator are available on their website
(https://lensstudio.snapchat.com/guides/submission/creating-an-icon/).

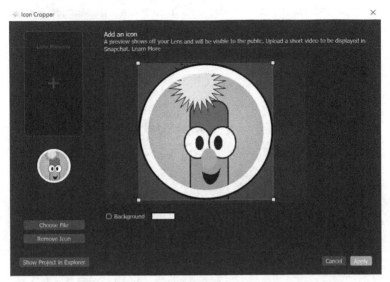

Let's now add a Lens Preview video.

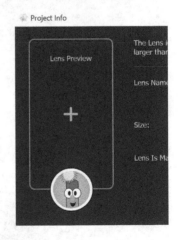

The preview video is another way to get people interested in trying your Lens. It actually gives them a live preview of what to expect when they're browsing in Lens Explorer. The process for getting a good preview used to be a lot more complicated, but the good folks on the

Lens Studio team really streamlined it so there's no excuse for not having a great preview. Select one from the standard model videos or record your own and upload it.

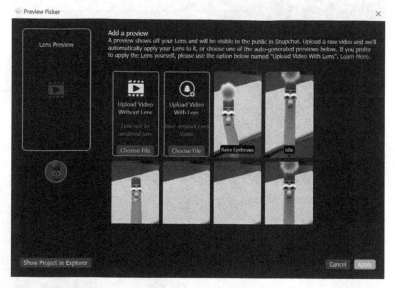

Now check everything over one last time to make sure everything is how you want it. And hit Apply.

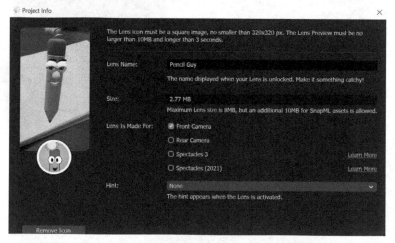

You're now at the very exciting moment where you're ready to hit that Publish Lens button and upload your masterpiece to Snapchat.

You'll get a status window letting you know the status of your upload. When it completes successfully, Lens Studio will open a browser window to walk you through the final part of the process.

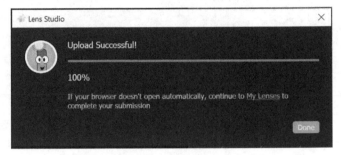

You'll be asked if you're Submitting a Business or Community Lens. Community Lenses stay on the platform for as long as you want and are free to everyone. The only time you'll submit a Business Lens is when a company with a Snapchat for Business account has hired you to build them one and you'll be adding it to their account.

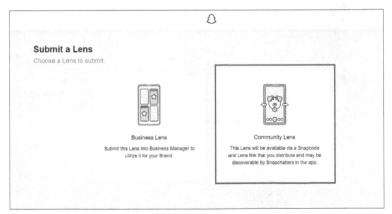

You'll next be asked if this is a new Lens or if you're updating an existing one. Select Submit New Lens.

You have one more step to submitting your lens, but it's a very important one if you want people to find your brilliant creation.

After double-checking your Preview video and the Lens Name, you'll definitely want to add some relevant meta tags and scan triggers. This will help Snapchat be able to send your Lens to Snapchatters who are looking for what you've made.

Finally, you can look at your visibility settings. Most of the time we want our Lenses to go Public right away, but there's other instances where we may be testing a feature or doing client work and we don't want everyone to see it. That's where the Hidden setting really comes in handy. You can submit a Hidden lens that only people with the URL or Snapcode can access.

Hit the Submit button and you're done! You'll get a victory screen and a link to go to the My Lenses management console.

In the Management console you can see that your newly submitted Lens is in review. In a little while you'll get an email that hopefully tells you your Lens is approved and out in the world.

Use it, share it with your friends, and post about it everywhere on social media! Congratulations!

Now that you've published at least one Lens (and hopefully much more soon), let's look around at the management console and see how we can control and gain deeper insights on our Lenses.

If you're not there already, go to https://my-lenses.snapchat.com/lenses.

Here we find a list of all the Lenses that we've submitted. As you can see, I've made too many to count. Each Lens is listed with its icon image, name, date modified, status, and buttons for Lens Link, insights, more options, to download Snapcode, or delete your Lens.

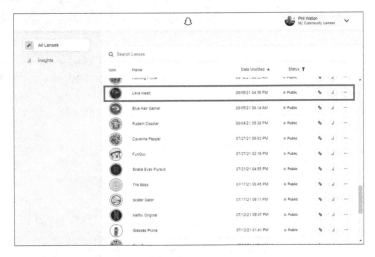

Each Lens has its own page for additional information. A few things to highlight here: your Lens ID is a unique code that helps the Snap team track down your Lens if for some reason you're interacting with tech support. You can change your Lens visibility here without uploading a new version of a Lens—which is great if you're wanting to privately test a Lens or you want to launch your latest on a certain day. You can also edit your Lens Tags and Scan Triggers if you weren't very inspired when you first uploaded and want to add some more. And you can also download your Snapcode here, which is great for sharing a visual

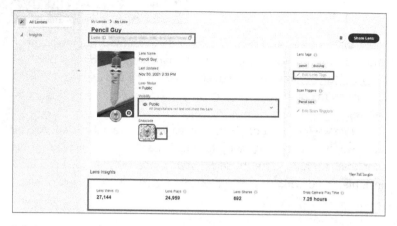

link to your creation.

Finally, one of my favorite things to look at is the Lens Insights. Here we can see how our Lens is performing with Snapchatters around the world.

> **Lens Views:** How many times people have watched a Snap with your Lens in it.
>
> **Lens Plays:** How many times people have opened and used your Lens.
>
> **Lens Shares:** How many times people have used your Lens in a Snap and sent it to someone else.
>
> **Snap Camera Play Time:** How long people have had your Lens active in Snap Camera.
>
> Clicking on the **View Full Insights** on a Lens page will take you to that Lens's individual analytics page.

LENS INSIGHTS

The Lens Insights page will give you a deeper look at how your Lenses are performing, both individually and collectively. Here we can get a picture of performance over the past seven days, twenty-eight days, or all time. Let's look at my own insights now.

Under the Audience section, we can see my Total Reach over the past month for my Lenses is at 19 million interactions but has declined 33.5 percent (I'd better finish this book and start making some new Lenses!). Total subscribers continue to slowly and steadily climb.

The demographics settings give me an idea for the age and gender breakdowns for my audience. About 70 percent are women and mostly young people. This gives me a better idea of the types of Lenses I can make to appeal to my audience—and probably not about 401(k)s or how to get rid of the gray in beards.

Top Countries and Top Interests lets me know which countries my audience is from and what they're interested in.

Going back to the top, when I look at the Engagement section, now I get a better look at performance over time for my Lenses. This shows how my Views, Plays, and Shares are trending. And there's a fourth tab that shows how many people are favoriting my Lenses.

And at the bottom we can see what our most popular Lenses

have been over the chosen time frame. Looks like people are really digging the Highway Stranger Lens—I love that one too!

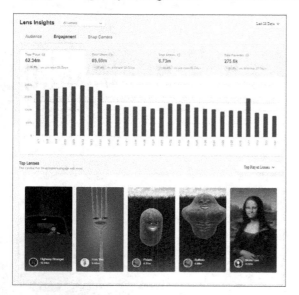

Finally, in the Snap Camera section, we can see the usage of my Lenses in Snap Camera over time. Looks like my Lenses are more popular during the week.

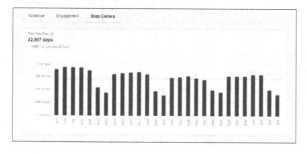

Remember that we can not only look at our overall lens insights, we can also look at individual Lenses as well by clicking on the dropdown and scrolling through or doing a search.

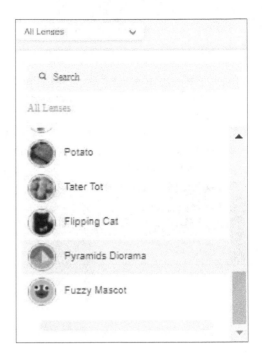

ENCOURAGEMENT

I have a final word about insights, audience, and getting your work seen. Believe me when I tell you that I know how hard it is starting off creating and not getting much traction. It can be easy to get discouraged when you're building Lens after Lens and getting only a couple thousand views. That was exactly where I started as well. I felt like I didn't know Lens Studio very well, like all my Lenses were basic, and that everyone else was way more talented than me. Even today, I still get those feelings.

But the best way to get through that is to keep creating, try new things, learn new skills, and connect to other creators who inspire you. If you keep pushing yourself and putting your best work out there, you'll find people who resonate with you and your Lenses.

You've already got your first fan right here—me!

ADDITIONAL LEARNING

Now that you know everything that I do about Lens Studio, you're probably hungry to learn more. Fortunately, there are plenty of great resources out there to help you become the next big name in AR experiences.

The first and most obvious place is the Lens Studio website. There are guides, templates, support, and a forum full of helpful people who want to keep you progressing on your AR journey.

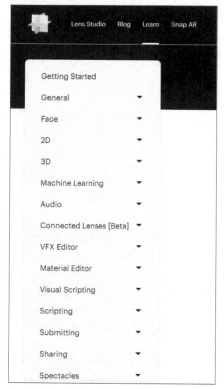

Snap also has the Snap AR YouTube channel (https://www.youtube.com/c/LensStudio), which has tons of great videos that not only teach you how to build but keep you up to date with the latest developments on the platform. They even offer live classes. Subscribe to the channel to learn more.

Another YouTube channel worth subscribing to is the talented Lens creator Ben Knutson (https://www.youtube.com/c/BenKnutson). He's super knowledgeable and has some great tutorials for beginners.

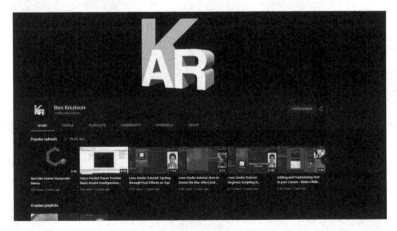

Mike Porter aka Models by Mike 3D (https://www.youtube.com/c/ ModelsbyMike3d) is another friend who is championing the cause of Lens creation for Snapchat. He's got a YouTube channel with helpful tutorials and he puts out a regular newsletter with tips and insights into the current state of the community. Check out his site https://arboot-camp.com/ for additional lessons to help you become an incredible AR creator.

Brandon Sears aka Apoc (https://www.youtube.com/user/D3ADL-3GEND) is constantly putting out incredible tutorials for all skill levels and features within Lens Studio.

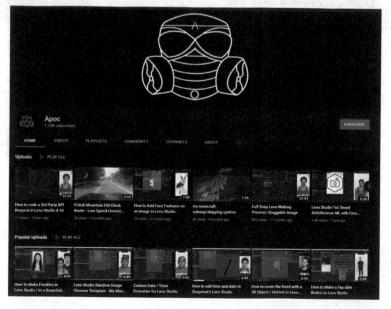

If you're interested in learning more about 3D, I definitely recommend starting with Blender YouTube. Get comfortable with the interface and get the grasp on building basic things. Just like with Lens Studio, here's a lot of the program to know, so take your time and have fun!

The great thing about Blender is that there's a lot of other people learning it as well, so there's plenty of YouTube tutorials out there. Everything from the most basic to the advanced. Start with their own official channel (youtube.com/c/BlenderFoundation).

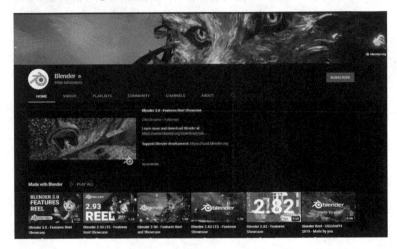

IN CONCLUSION

Well, we did it! We've successfully built several complete AR experiences that showcase a variety of Snapchat Lens types. The skills and techniques you've learned through this process can be remixed and combined in many ways to produce endless possibilities. I'm so excited to see what you create! Thank you for joining me on this journey. I truly believe that augmented reality will fundamentally change our lives in the coming years with advancements in technology. You are on the ground for that revolution. Let's go!

ACKNOWLEDGMENTS

I would like to give my sincere thanks and deepest gratitude to the Snap Lens Studio team for their time, attention, and generosity over the entire time I've been in the process of becoming a better AR creator. They are true champions for this medium and are always pushing the boundaries of what's possible. Thank you specifically to Kaitlyn Benitez-Strine for her tireless work and encouragement on this book.

Thank you as well to my fellow Snapchat Lens creators and the creator community. You challenge and inspire me to work hard and learn new skills. Your friendship and camaraderie have made building Lenses on Snapchat a true joy.

I give thanks to the many fans of my work over the years as well. If you've ever used one of my Lenses to make a silly video and shared it with a friend, that's the greatest thing I could ask.

Finally, I'd like to thank the people who helped me directly or indirectly in the creation of this book: Tiffani Sahara, Cyrene Quiamco, Sallia Goldstein, Dustin Ballard, Ben Knutson, Mike Porter, Brandon Sears, Carey Nelson Burch Leo, Marisa Munoz. And let's not forget my wonderful family—my strange, creative daughters who give me the most unique Lens ideas, and my incredible, supportive wife, whom I'm constantly inflicting new ideas upon to the ever-encouraging refrain of "That's great, hon."

Thank you!

ABOUT THE AUTHOR

While his Potato Snapchat Lens gets all the glory, Phil Walton has spent years working in storytelling and creative 3D art. After serving in the Air Force, Phil returned to school to study animation and after ten years as a 3D character animator, found new opportunities in the realm of augmented reality. His distinctive Snapchat Lenses have been viewed around the world over five and a half billion times and he was recently selected to be a Snap AR Creator Ambassador, advocating for education, conversation, and creation for the Snap Lens Network community. His augmented reality work has appeared on the Super Bowl pregame show, *Saturday Night Live*, *The Late Late Show with James Corden*, *The Late Show with Jimmy Kimmel*, music videos, viral tweets, Twitch Streams, and countless TikToks. Phil is also the lead AR developer, creating the unique augmented reality characters on the TV show, Nickelodeon's Unfiltered. He lives in Tennessee and can be found on his various social media channels.

Snapchat @phillip.walton

Instagram @phillip.walton

Twitter @fireandknife

Phillipwalton.com

Don't miss Phil's other book, *The Ultimate Guide to Snapchat*, where he teaches you everything you need to know about the app your Lenses will be displayed on, and which is the perfect companion book to this one. It's available from Turner Publishing or wherever awesome books are sold.